HOMETOWN HEROES

Successful Deaf Youth in America

Diane Robinette

Kendall Green Publications
Gallaudet University Press
Washington, D.C.

Kendall Green Publications
An imprint of Gallaudet University Press
Washington, DC 20002

Library of Congress Cataloging-in-Publication Data

Robinette, Diane. 1951-
   Hometown heroes : successful deaf youth in America /
Diane Robinette.
       p.   cm.
   Summary : Profiles of forty-four deaf youth who are succeeding in life
and fulfilling their goals.
   ISBN 0-930323-69-6 : $11.95
   1. Children, Deaf — United States — Biography — Juvenile literature.
[1. Deaf. 2. Physically handicapped.] I. Title. II. Title : Hometown heroes.
HV2534.A3R63   1990
362.4'2'092273—dc20
[B]   90-4729
[920]   CIP
                                            AC

CONTENTS

PREFACE

This book has two purposes. First, to encourage young deaf people to reach out and aim for what they want in life. And, second, to inform hearing readers about the wide variety of interests and skills that deaf people possess.

The young people in this book have two characteristics in common — a hearing loss and a supportive family. The importance of supportive parents and other family members cannot be overemphasized. This support, while not directly stated in all instances, is crucial to the success of these young people.

These students are saying: "Recognize *me*. Recognize my skills and talents instead of focusing on my hearing loss." All of them have faced challenges and, at one time or another, have had to take the initiative in educating hearing people about their accomplishments, feelings, problems, and needs. Frequently, they needed an extra measure of patience and perseverance to achieve the success they wanted. Some have pointed out that they have had to work harder than their hearing peers to achieve this success. And when this success is achieved, they want to acknowledge it themselves and have it recognized by others. Some acknowledge that they have received inspiration from God. The desire shared by these young people to help others indicates that they are interested in service, not stardom. They have been successful not because they have earned trophies, awards, and applause, but because they have developed the self-esteem necessary to recognize their capabilities.

This book began as a questionnaire sent to teachers and administrators listed in the *American Annals of the Deaf Annual Survey of Schools and Classes for the Deaf in the*

United States. I received 130 responses to my initial questionnaires. I formatted the information from the questionnaires and the students' autobiographies into a profile about each student and then sent the profiles back to the students for their approval. Then, I wrote more drafts until the students and I arrived at the final copy. Gallaudet University Press did additional editorial work on the articles.

In writing this book, I was dependent on the generosity of the young people and their parents. As a hearing person, I am an outsider to Deaf culture even though I have taught deaf and hearing children and young people for 14 years. Therefore, I am most appreciative of the willingness of these young people to share their insights and experiences with me. Getting to know them through letters and phone calls has been a gratifying and rewarding experience.

This book is but a brief glimpse into the lives of a few young people who are facing the challenges before them willingly and courageously. Undoubtedly, they will continue to mature into the leaders of the next generation.

I am indebted to the following people for their encouragement, advice, and assistance in preparing the manuscript: Dr. and Mrs. Louis Ball; Mrs. Marlene Bomgardner; Miss Susan Childress; Mr. and Mrs. Jon Eargle; Mrs. Sue Fann; Mrs. Jenny Fowler; Miss Carolyn Fraser; Dr. Angie Fryer; Mr. and Mrs. Mark Hamrick; Mrs. Ronda Hickerson; Mrs. Jean LaForest; Dr. and Mrs. Herbert Miles; Miss Kim Miller; Mrs. Sherry Moran; Mrs. Kathryne Nowell; Miss Karen Robinette; Miss Reba Robinette; Miss Becky Sue Rodgers; Mrs. Rachel Schlafer-Parton; Miss Anna Seale; Dr. Jerry Seale; Mrs. Ann Trudel; Dr. Olga Welch.

INTRODUCTION

Terrylene
**Actress
Chicago, Illinois
Model Secondary
School for the Deaf
Washington, D.C.
Class of 1984**

Because you and I are deaf, we understand what it's like to be deaf. Our people have a history of struggle — a struggle to define ourselves and to tell the world who we are. The world assumes that it knows us. This struggle has given us a foundation from which to grow. We have to explain our desire to be seen as individuals and to be respected as a culture. This will continue to be difficult and challenging, but let us not pause on our journey.

I am a young girl dreaming of becoming an actress. I sneak into the bathroom and lock the door. I sign whatever comes from my imagination in front of the mirror. Then comes a loud knock — not a light, "hearing" knock, but a thunderously loud "deaf" knock — that shakes the walls. It scares me back to reality. I open the door and pretend that I have a stomachache.

Soon, I am entertaining my mother's company on an imaginary stage in our living room. Everyone smiles and laughs at my wild desire to act. Their eyes say, "Cute little girl, your dreams are bigger than reality." I am so busy performing that I don't see this message hidden in their eyes.

Now, I am seven years old and my deaf parents send me to an oral school. (There are no residential schools for the deaf in the area.) My brother and I keep forgetting that we are *not* to sign. Here we are again in the principal's office, sitting on our hands or standing with our noses to the wall.

Entering a new school again, I give my first performance in the mainstream program at Taft School in Orange County, California. This time, I am allowed to sign, but only in Signing Exact English (SEE). I'm not a great SEE signer but I sign my first song, "Sunshine On My Shoulders," in front of a real audience. The lights are very bright and they shine right into my eyes. Those weird, black shapes that look like ocean waves are really the heads of people in the audience.

I am nine years old and living at the Texas School for the Deaf. I make my first appearance using my native language — American Sign Language. Peeking through the curtain, I see that *too many* people have come to see the show! I am scared but I manage to remember my first line. (To this day, stage fright still creeps up on me. But I'm always safe when I remember my first line.) I sign a piece Ms. Krusmark helped me create — about sunshine and rain and rainbows.

At twelve, I'm leaving the California School for the Deaf in Berkeley and heading back to Chicago, my hometown. I go to a mainstream program in a public school again. It's tougher this time. In junior high, people don't hide the message in their eyes. They just say, "For you, acting is ridiculous!" I feel lost, doubting my dreams. I turn to poetry to relieve my doubts.

Now I am a mainstreamed freshman in a public high school. "You can't do it. . . . We have enough people. . . . I need taller girls on the basketball team. . . . There's no interpreter available. . . . You need to speak better. . . . I don't know what to do with you." No matter what I achieve, "deaf" is stamped across my forehead. I sit back quietly and wonder why. I need to understand that no one knows all the answers.

I realize I need to change schools. During my sophomore year, I enter the Model Secondary School for the Deaf in Washington, D.C. At last, the door to the theater is open to me. I am given opportunities, choices, and support. This is the beginning of realizing my dream. Commitment, discipline, and hard work are what make my dream come true.

I continue to work on achieving my dream. I *am* an actress, living in Los Angeles and working in my chosen profession. I want to continue to grow and improve, not only as an actress, but as a person.

My dream is still expanding. But one dream being realized will not cure the problems that others face. By fulfilling your dream to be what you believe you can be — scientist, politician, painter, astronaut, welder, dancer, environmentalist — you and I will dispel the stereotypes associated with deafness. By taking the time to educate ourselves, we learn patience. By educating others, we share our uniqueness.

This book and others like it will create an opening for friends, parents, relatives, physicians, and people like ourselves to encourage our dreams. One day, we will all come together and respect each other's diversity.

Television guest star appearance on "Cagney and Lacey." Played a recurring role in the television series "Beauty and the Beast." Toured Europe in Godspell. Played Sarah in Children of a Lesser God at Fulton Opera House.

HOMETOWN HEROES

Successful Deaf Youth in America

East

BOBBY FULLER

ALICE ANN MCNULTY

RODNEY BOMGARDNER

LENNY FISHER

LISA CICCARELLI

LYNNE CICCARELLI

IVETTE BELLANCA

MARY SLACK

INDRANI HEWSEN

ROBERT GORDON FULLER

Varsity Soccer Champ Eyes Career in Science

Bobby

**Lakeville, Massachusetts
Boston School for the Deaf and Randolph High School
Randolph, Massachusetts
Class of 1988**

I want to be a scientist. I have had four years of science—earth science, biology, chemistry, and physics. Chemistry is my favorite. I enjoy solving problems.

Boston School for the Deaf (BSD) and Randolph High School (RHS) have a parallel-path program for hearing-impaired students. I have tutors, notetakers, interpreters, and classes for the deaf taught by BSD teachers. But I take all my courses at RHS because I am a mainstreamed student. I really enjoy my classes. They move along faster and cover more material than classes for deaf students.

I am on the honor roll and a member of the National Honor Society. This year I am a senior. I am class vice president, Student Council treasurer, and yearbook business manager.

I love gymnastics, too. I have been taking gymnastics for three years and I participate in every event—the parallel bar, high bar, rings, floor exercise, pommel horse, and vault. My favorite events are pommel horse and vault. Pommel horse is the most difficult event in men's gymnastics because it requires near-perfect balance, strength, flexibility, and graceful movements. Vaulting is fun. It's a terrific, powerful feeling to leap over the vault.

For five years, I have played on the varsity soccer team. I play left wing, right wing, and halfback. In 1984, 1985, and 1987, our team won the New England Schools for the Deaf Soccer Championship. In 1986, I was named most improved player.

I enjoy other sports, too—biking, swimming, and cross-country skiing. In the summer, I ride my bike ten miles a day. I am an excellent swimmer. I learned to ski when I was eight years old. We have not had enough snow recently for cross-country skiing, but I enjoy downhill skiing, too.

At the Lutheran Church of the Way, I serve as treasurer of my youth group. In 1986, I went to the Missouri Synod Youth Gathering in Washington, D.C. Of the 15,000 youths there from all over the United

States and Canada, ten of us were deaf. I was glad we had an interpreter.

At the conference, I accepted Jesus Christ as my savior. Now I read the Bible and try to grow closer to my Lord. The Bible is hard to understand, but I am learning a little more each day.

The most unforgettable experience of my life was a family vacation in Europe. We went to France, England, Belgium, and The Netherlands. Paris was my favorite place. I loved it, especially at night when it was filled with lights.

When I was standing in the gardens near the Eiffel Tower, a Frenchwoman tapped me on the shoulder. I turned around and she spoke to me quickly in French. I know a little French and practiced some in Paris, but I couldn't understand that woman! She realized I was a foreigner when I told her I spoke English. What fun to be mistaken for a Frenchman!

I wanted to take French in school, but I was not allowed. That won't stop me, though. I plan to take it later—when I enter Gallaudet University. I like languages and I study French, Russian, and Spanish in my leisure time.

In eighth grade, I volunteered to help at the Trailside Museum, a museum about wildlife. It was my job to take care of the animals. That spring I taught deaf students at my school about the animals at that museum.

During my sophomore and junior years, I was involved with the Boston Theatre of the Deaf. My deaf and hearing classmates gathered together to learn theatre skills. The deaf students taught the hearing students sign language. They learned fast and seemed to want to learn more. In one production, I played the role of a man who watches his own funeral. It was a successful play.

I look forward to entering Gallaudet University. My goals are to become a science teacher for hearing-impaired students and also teach gymnastics.

I want to tell all deaf students not to give up easily. Keep doing the things that interest you.

I wanted to take French in school, but I was not allowed. That won't stop me, though. I plan to take it later— when I enter Gallaudet University."

Loving Cats—and their Humans

Alice Ann

**Sellersville,
Pennsylvania
Pennridge High
School
Sellersville,
Pennsylvania
Class of 1990**

Photograph by John Garner,
Perkasie *News Herald*,
Perkasie, PA.

I love cats," said Alice Ann McNulty, a student at Pennridge High School in Sellersville, Pennsylvania. "They are gentle, playful, easy to take care of, and small enough to sleep on your lap."

Alice Ann knows what she's talking about. She has five cats, Cinderella, Alicia, Bambi, Joshua, and Kerry. She has had cats, each with its own personality, for most of her life.

"My first cat was black," remembered Alice Ann. "I used to dress him up in a diaper and a dress. He slept with me."

"One day I thought he was sick, so I tried to take his temperature with a thermometer. The thermometer broke, and mom had to take him to the vet. He wasn't sick at all!"

Taking care of cats, observing them, and loving them has helped Alice Ann to understand more about life. It has given her courage.

"When I first became a teenager, I wanted to be hearing," said Alice Ann. "I was frustrated."

Then came Midnight, a tiny kitten who faced the world fearlessly without ever seeing it. Midnight was blind.

"He would sit on my shoulder while I worked in the garden," said Alice Ann. "When I leaned over, he would move halfway down my back to keep his balance."

Midnight would ride around on everyone, even climbing onto the shoulders of visitors.

"Guests were surprised when they became Midnight's perch," she said. "That cat wasn't afraid of anything. He inspired me to face the world, too, and ignore my problems."

Besides being busy with her feline friends, Alice Ann is active in Girl Scouts. She received the Juliet Gordon Lowe Statue for ten consecutive years of Girl Scouting. She earned sixty merit badges, helped her troop with fund-raisers, helped out in a nursing home, and attended a leadership weekend with the senior Girl Scouts at Freedom Valley. In 1985, she earned the Silver Merit Award.

"Next year, I start to work toward the Gold Award," she said. "To earn this award, I must work on a project of special interest to me. I really admire my present Girl Scout leader and appreciate all that she has done for me. She is the person that I most want to be like."

The Gold Award is the highest award given in Girl Scouting.

Alice Ann is very active in school, too. She was a member at-large of the Student Council during her freshman year.

"I enjoy sharing my ideas with the other students," she said.

Encouraged by her dad and her seventh-grade shop teacher, Alice Ann took up woodworking and other crafts, and became the only girl in the school's freshman shop class. She made a hat rack, a coat rack, and a car license plate that said "I love cats."

A junior, Alice Ann is mainstreamed with ten other hearing-impaired students who are bused to the school from all over the county. Alice Ann reports that she really enjoys all her classes—mostly because of the teachers.

"My teachers have really contributed greatly to my self-esteem," she said. "They have a wonderful, caring attitude and a terrific sense of humor. They have been very special to me. I would never have been able to learn without their help."

The hearing-impaired students have homeroom together and then are main-streamed into as many "hearing classes" as they can handle. Alice Ann goes to classes in the high school in the morning and then studies agriculture and horticulture in the afternoon at the vocational school.

Working with plants and animals is Alice Ann's specialty—and she has been very successful in it. In her sophomore year, her entries placed second, third, and fourth in the school agricultural fair. She entered her own farm-grown vegetables, baked goods, a colored sand design, a corsage, and a dried floral wreath.

Alice Ann was elected treasurer of the Future Farmers of America (FFA). She was the top salesperson in the FFA Easter ham sale. She also participated in the Home, Farm, and Flower Show, entering a bee display, hydroponic plants, baked goods, a dolphin topiary hanging plant, and a cactus dish garden. Also, she worked on learning to shear her ram and training her sheep to show in the ring.

Alice Ann is active in her Baptist church, too. She goes to Bible study with her deaf friends. They have other activities, also, such as bowling and trips to museums.

In 1987, Alice Ann went to the Bill Rice Ranch Camp for the Deaf, a Christian camp in Tennessee.

"I was surprised how much it meant to me," she said. "Deaf people were every-where. Everyone was signing—even people who worked in the stores."

Her goals are to become a teacher of deaf students, a veterinarian, or a computer programmer. She also hopes to have a family.

"I want to be a friend," she said, "and touch all people with caring and love."

Taking care of cats, observing them, and loving them has helped Alice Ann to understand more about life. It has given her courage.

Wrestler Gets Firm Hold on Life

Rodney

**Annville,
Pennsylvania
Annville-Cleona
High School
Annville,
Pennsylvania
Class of 1989**

Since he was a little boy, Rodney Bomgardner, a student at Annville-Cleona High School, in Annville, Pennsylvania, has milked cows, worked in the fields, and helped with the livestock on his family's farm. His knowledge of farming is so extensive that, even when Rodney was a small child, his hearing clinician did not know all the words Rodney used to describe his farm chores. Finally Rodney advised her to get a brown notebook, like the one she had given him for his vocabulary words, to make a list of his "farm words." And she did just that.

Rodney has been a member of 4-H since he was eight years old. He raises a steer and eight to twelve hogs every year for 4-H projects. He often takes his animals to the Pennsylvania State Farm Show where he has won three Showmanship trophies, three Fitter (grooming) trophies, one Reserve Champion Hog trophy, and four Reserve Champion Steer trophies.

As a Future Farmers of America (FFA)

member, Rodney has won awards for beef and swine proficiency and meat judging. He won a second-place award at the state level for his record book. Rodney has been vice president of his FAA chapter and was elected county sentinel.

At the Lebanon Area Fair, Rodney won several trophies for garden-tractor pulling. He also won first- and second-place tractor-pulling awards using the family's International Harvester 1206.

Rodney has earned his share of academic success. In third grade, he became the first hearing-impaired student in his school district to be mainstreamed. He began communicating exclusively by speaking and speechreading. In tenth grade, classmates tutored him in American culture, while Rodney tutored them in algebra and art.

"It was fun to be able to help each other," Rodney said.

His efforts were rewarded when he was inducted into the National Honor Society. This was an important milestone for Rodney.

Rodney loves sports. His first classroom

My parents have encouraged me and my classmates have accepted me. I feel that I can succeed in any career I choose."

teacher was the daughter of Bud Grant, the former Minnesota Vikings' head coach. Rodney has been interested in football and other sports ever since. Rodney's father, who coaches Little League in his community, encourages him.

"My dad taught me to love trout fishing, deer hunting, and collecting International Harvester memorabilia, too," Rodney said.

Rodney is a wrestler. He placed first in the midget weight class the first time he participated in a tournament. He continued wrestling, earning a bronze medal in the 165-pound weight class at the Elizabethtown Optimist Tourney, as well as his school's "most improved player" plaque. In 1986, he entered the Strongman Competition at his school for the first time and took fourth place, a sophomore competing with seniors.

Art is Rodney's favorite subject. The oil painting he did for his art class won first place in one local contest and second in another. Entitled "Pine Creek," the painting depicts one of Rodney's favorite fishing spots near Pennsylvania's Grand Canyon. The next oil he did—of Hereford cattle in a pasture—won Best of Show.

"My parents have encouraged me and my classmates have accepted me," said Rodney. "I feel that I can succeed in any career I choose."

Rodney is not sure yet what his career will be, but he is considering going into agriculture.

"I'm disappointed that many programs for deaf students do not offer studies in agriculture," he said. "I have a dream of bringing agriculture into the learning experiences of deaf students."

Rodney believes in facing life with the attitude his father told him to adopt when wrestling more experienced boys.

"My dad told me to give the other guy a struggle. Make him earn that pin. Don't give in," Rodney said.

"Life is like that. We can't give up without a struggle. And we must give our best. Sometimes our best turns out to be better than we thought."

Speaking Up in the Present

Lenny

**Stevenson, Maryland
Parkville Senior
High School
Baltimore, Maryland
Class of 1987**

My bar mitzvah was a highlight of my life. I read aloud in Hebrew from the scriptures in front of the whole synagogue. I studied for many years to be able to read the Hebrew language and answer questions about my faith. After I finished, the whole congregation praised me for standing up and speaking.

I always speak. I use the oral method of communication, speaking and speechreading, to talk with other people. I have worked on speaking and speechreading since I was three years old. It is difficult for me to understand some people whose lips are hard to read. But I am able to talk and communicate with hearing people.

At Parkville Senior High School in Baltimore, Maryland, where I was a student, school was quite difficult. For some classes I had notetakers, but otherwise I was on my own. I took business law, Latin, principles of accounting, Constitution, public issues, journalism, and algebra, among other classes. Algebra was my favorite subject because I liked the challenge of solving problems. An itinerant teacher helped me once a week because I didn't have time to take resource.

My teachers were very helpful and I am grateful to them. I maintained a B+ average during my senior year and made the honor roll every quarter.

During the summer, I worked as a camp counselor for children with hearing problems and learning problems. It was hard to control their behavior. Once, a camper wandered away from his bunk and we spent an hour looking for him. We finally found him in the woods. The campers were friendly, though, and generally very helpful.

Last summer, I traveled to London and Paris with my family. I was astonished to see all the famous buildings of those famous cities—Big Ben, Parliament, Buckingham Palace (where we saw the colorful changing of the guard), the Eiffel Tower, Notre Dame, the Louvre, the Arch of Triumph, and the Palace of Versailles. We saw the tomb of Napoleon, too.

Now I am a full-time student at Catonsville Community College and a part-time worker in the county library. I like working in the library because it helps me to increase my knowledge of books. Also, I can help other people. For example, one day when I was shelving books, a woman came to me and asked, "Where do I find books about dogs?" I guided her to the right section. I felt proud to be able to help her.

I am now working toward an associate's degree in accounting at Catonsville Community College because I have a good knowledge of math and enjoy solving problems. I may go to the University of Baltimore to get my B.S. degree.

Ten years from now, I hope to own a home and be married with at least two children and several cats. I hope to be working as an accountant in a widely known firm. I would like to have my own office, too, so people can come to me with financial problems. I also want to work as a volunteer for an animal rights group.

It is very important for deaf people to socialize so they have friends to support them. Being deaf doesn't mean that an individual is totally different from hearing people. We have to adapt to our problem and strive to do our best.

Our future awaits.

I *always speak. I always use the oral method of communication, speaking and speechreading, to talk with other people. I have worked on speaking and speechreading since I was three years old."*

LISA MARIE CICCARELLI

Clubs Lead Way to Self-Confidence

Lisa

**Strasburg,
Pennsylvania
Lampeter-Strasburg
High School
Lampeter,
Pennsylvania
Class of 1985**

Lisa Marie Ciccarelli, from Strasburg, Pennsylvania, developed confidence in herself by joining clubs and teams. In high school, she played basketball, softball, and field hockey. She received outstanding player certificates in basketball, playing the position of forward.

Lisa joined the Future Business Leaders of America (FBLA) and the American Field Service (AFS). When she attended the Regional Conference of Business and competed in office procedures, she placed third.

"I was pleased," she said. "It made me happy to make it almost to the top. I love to meet a challenge and explore new areas to find out what I can and cannot do."

Lisa was mainstreamed full-time through high school.

"I was kind of stubborn and said I didn't need interpreters," she remembered. "But I did use notetakers and I had a tutor three times a week."

She also felt embarrassed about people seeing her hearing aid. But, starting college, she found that it bothered her less.

Lisa entered Bloomsburg University's Summer Career Academic Development program in preparation for fall classes.

"I was confused at first," she said of her first college semester. "I started to major in elementary education for the hearing impaired and then changed to health science. Then I talked to people who were social work majors. Social work seemed interesting to me, because I love dealing with people."

So Lisa changed her major to social work. This time she finally began to feel that she was in classes that were right for her.

"College is a big change from high school," she said. "The professors often turn their backs to write on the chalkboard, and I miss part of their lecture and feel lost. So I requested interpreters for all my classes. They clarify hard words for me and help me participate in class. It has worked out just fine."

Lisa continues to use notetakers, too. She takes most of her tests in the professors' offices so that she is not distracted when other students, who tend to finish before she does, leave while she is still working.

In college, Lisa has continued to stay involved in clubs and outside-of-class activities. She joined the Bicycle Club during her junior year. The members work hard in the weight room and then go riding. Also, Lisa participates in retreats sponsored by the Catholic Campus Ministry.

"Retreats offer me a nice time to pray and make friends," she said. "I encouraged one of my friends to come with me, and she enjoyed the experience, too."

One of Lisa's club experiences became a source of frustration. She became president of the Bloomsburg Association of the Hearing Impaired, a club for deaf and hard-of-hearing students.

"I had many problems because some of the other officers did not fulfill their duties," she said. "I felt that I had not succeeded in my job."

A more experienced person from another school helped her out. Then Lisa was chosen vice president of the club.

"That was a relief," she said. "I enjoy being active in the club, but this way I do not have all the responsibility."

Lisa hopes to continue her education and eventually earn a master's degree in counseling for the deaf.

"I want to get a job counseling families," she said. "Each family is unique and I want to help guide parents and teenagers in any way I can."

Lisa and her sister, Lynne, are the only two deaf members of their hearing family. Lisa said that she believes it is important that deaf people interact with hearing people—and that hearing people interact with deaf people.

"I would like to see employers give their employees the opportunity to learn sign language," she said. "Sign language is a form of art to me. Learning it is like learning a foreign language."

Lisa said that she believes that other deaf young people should follow her example and try to be active in clubs and activities.

"It helps you feel more comfortable—less self-conscious about your deafness," she stated. "Challenge yourself and get out there! Be involved in clubs and sports."

I would like to see employers give their employees the opportunity to learn sign language. Sign language is a form of art to me. Learning it is like learning a foreign language."

Youth Leader Explores Many Cultures

Lynne

**Strasburg,
Pennsylvania
Lampeter-Strasburg
High School
Lampeter,
Pennsylvania
Class of 1987**

Lynne Ann Ciccarelli believes in involvement just like her older sister Lisa, who is also deaf. She joined her high school chapter of the Junior National Association of the Deaf (Jr. NAD) and was elected vice president and treasurer.

The Jr. NAD collected clothes for poor people and sponsored a Dance-a-thon to collect money for the Leukemia Foundation. Lynne traveled to Georgia to attend a Jr. NAD conference, where she attended meetings on business and leadership, and befriended deaf students from all over the United States.

Lynne joined the American Field Service (AFS), a club with a strong interest in promoting understanding among cultures. With AFS, Lynne traveled to Maryland, lived with another AFS member in her home for one week, and, for one day, attended school with her hostess. She also visited Washington, D.C.

Lynne was involved with the Future Business Leaders of America, which helps students get involved in the business world. She won third place in the Regional Data Processing Contest.

"I was the only deaf student in the club," said Lynne. "I felt honored and the experience gave me confidence."

In 1987, Lynne received the Optimist Award. Each year, the Optimist Club honors a deaf student who shows optimism in daily life. Lynne made a prizewinning speech and the Optimists awarded her money, which she is using for her college education.

Lynne, a Catholic, is also active in her church. She enjoys attending religious classes and occasionally goes on weekend retreats with her family.

Lynne was a cheerleader. And she enjoys traveling.

"I visited Puerto Rico," she said. "and learned how their culture differs from ours. How simply they live! Their diet and the crops they grow were especially different and interesting to me."

Lynne has also traveled to Maine where

her sister lives, to Disney World and Sea World in Florida, and to Annapolis, Maryland, for another sister's graduation from the U.S. Naval Academy. "The ceremony was very impressive," Lynne stated.

Now a student at the National Technical Institute for the Deaf (NTID) in Rochester, N.Y., Lynne is working on an associate's degree, concentrating on acquiring secretarial skills. She is continuing her involvement in clubs, too, by belonging to a student government club called Ellingson, Peterson, Bell.

"The club has enabled me to make a lot of friends and develop my leadership skills," she said.

In the future, Lynne wants to get married, have children, and hold down two jobs. She wants to be a secretary for an insurance company and own a beauty salon that provides hair care for deaf customers.

"Deaf people can be anything they want to be as long as they are willing to try hard," she said. "I want to serve the deaf and hearing communities in whatever area I am needed."

Lynne's advice to other deaf teens is simple. "Never give up," she said. "Always think positive. Be optimistic!"

I visited Puerto Rico and learned how their culture differs from ours. How simply they live! Their diet and the crops they grow were especially different and interesting to me."

Camping, Reading, Traveling, and Laughing A Lot

Ivette

Howell, New Jersey
Model Secondary School for the Deaf
Washington, D.C.
Class of 1988

Being alone in the woods makes me feel whole and in harmony with nature. I love camping and hiking. My uncle has woods next to his home in New York State. When I camp out there, I sleep in a wooden shack that my uncle built himself and eat food that has been cooked over a campfire, including burned marshmallows. The most beautiful part of the woods is the waterfall. It has a water slide formed by natural rock.

I was a counselor at a Jewish day camp and I learned a lot from the experience. I learned about the history and religion of the Jewish people and how to work with young children and my hearing peers. We sang Hebrew and American camp songs, swam in the pool, did arts and crafts, talked, played games, and, best of all, laughed a lot.

I worked with the small children and sometimes they really surprised me. We were playing tag one day, and I chased and tagged a few children. That was easy!

Then I tried to tag one five-year-old boy. He zigzagged and sprinted away from me whenever I got close to him. When I learned that pattern, he changed it and ran loops. Finally I stopped. "You won!" I told him. And I smiled.

Working with the other teenagers, who were all hearing, wasn't easy. I had to be assertive and ask many questions. It was important for me to tell them that I was hard-of-hearing. Then things worked out well.

At the Model Secondary School for the Deaf (MSSD), in Washington, D.C., where I go to school, I have made the honor roll several times. I also joined the peer advisor program. In this program, students learn to be assertive, polite, attentive, and helpful. We serve as counselors for other students who have minor problems in the dorm or at school. I try to be a good role model. I enjoy it. It helps me a lot.

As a sophomore, I was chosen Best Rookie of the Year. I received this honor because I learned sign language quickly, got to know the students and staff, and adjusted well to life at MSSD.

My counselor sponsored a Women's Group and I became a member. We discussed topics such as our different backgrounds and cultures, our bodies, our fear of being harassed, and our feelings about boys. Often we invited female guests to come and discuss their experiences and give us advice.

In 1987, I went to Carrara, a small city in Italy, to visit my grandfather, uncles, aunts, and cousins who still live there.

We traveled a lot, visiting many different places. We went to islands, beaches, and mountains. We visited castles and attended festivals and concerts. Italy's narrow cobblestone streets and old-fashioned buildings fascinated me. I only regret not knowing the Italian language. It would have made my visit so much more enjoyable.

One of my favorite hobbies is reading. I enjoy reading about American Indians, psychology, philosophy, and Christianity.

Also, I read self-help books on how to be positive. Books make my life brighter.

I want to attend the National Technical Institute for the Deaf and I would like to have a career where I can travel. I would like to take pictures all over the world. I am especially interested in newly discovered ancient cities, tribal peoples who have not had contact with the modern world, and the national parks in the United States.

I would like to marry a man who is deaf or hard-of-hearing. I want to have one child and adopt another. My dream is to live in the mountains of Colorado, near a waterfall.

I would strongly encourage deaf students to do their best in school. Try to be friendly with the teachers. They have feelings, too. It is not easy being a teacher for this generation!

Try a small experiment. Go to your parents and close friends and ask them why they like or love you. That should help you to love yourself. Suddenly the world will look better.

Working with the other teenagers, who were all hearing, wasn't easy. I had to be assertive and ask many questions. It was important for me to tell them that I was hard-of-hearing."

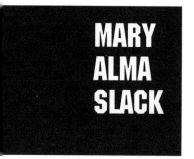

"New World" Opens for Talented Island Student in America

Mary

**St. Kitts,
West Indies
Model Secondary
School for the
Deaf
Washington, D.C.
Class of 1988**

In 1985, Mary Alma Slack left her native island of St. Kitts in the West Indies to come to America. She entered the Model Secondary School for the Deaf (MSSD), in Washington, D.C., and "a whole new world opened up" for her. Mary did well in academics and theatre, won prizes for her art, and was elected Miss MSSD. When her parents flew up to see her graduate in 1988, they were proud to see their daughter presented with a special award as the student who best displayed the spirit of the school. Here is an interview with Mary.

How were you educated on St. Kitts?

I learned from my mother first. She enrolled in the John Tracey Clinic correspondence course to learn how to teach me to talk. Later, I went to a small local school for the deaf that operates for three hours a day.

How long did you go to that school?

Until fourth grade, when my parents asked the principal of a Catholic school to allow me to enter that school. Being mainstreamed was tough, but I worked hard and was promoted every year. When I reached tenth grade, though, it was difficult for me to keep up with the class.

Why did you come to America?

My parents prayed for a school where I could complete my high school studies and socialize with other deaf students. They learned about MSSD and sent me there. A whole new world opened up for me.

Did you get homesick?

Oh, yes, I got very homesick! But my dorm "mom" helped me a lot. And Martin and Cecelia Alexander took me as their foster child. The Alexanders and their eight children have shown me so much love. "Aunt" Cecelia and "Uncle" Martin have been like real parents to me.

How did you do at MSSD?

I worked hard and got good grades. I was on the honor roll several times. The teachers also gave me special recognition for my potential as an actress and dancer.

Have you performed on stage?

I was a member of the cast for two drama productions—*Quest* and *Broken Promises*. I also participated in several dance concerts, *Wing Formation*, *The Spanish Dance*, and *The Ballroom Dance.* We performed musical interpretations of "Memory" and "Sisters," too. I was a mime in *Trick and Trunk*.

What was your favorite subject?

Mathematics. I am really motivated to work with numbers in some way. I would like to become a bookkeeper or an accountant.

What were some of your other activities at MSSD?

I volunteered for many activities. I gave tours of our campus and assisted new students. I was a peer advisor and then a senior peer advisor. I also joined the computer club, played defense on the girls' intramural flag football team, and played on the volleyball intramural team. I also worked as a mail clerk in the general post office, sorting mail, typing bills, and doing some bookkeeping.

Has your family been helpful?

Yes! I have a beautiful family. They prayed for me to earn a scholarship for Gallaudet University's preparatory program, and I did! But they still must save money to pay for the rest of my college expenses and for my ticket home each summer. It's very costly.

What are your future goals?

I want to continue working hard so that I will be able to graduate from Gallaudet Univer-

I *am really motivated to work with numbers in some way. I would like to become a bookkeeper or an accountant."*

sity and get a good job. I may go back to St. Kitts, my homeland, and become a teacher, counselor, or social worker with the deaf. I hope that I will be able to help the deaf community when I return home.

Do you have any advice for deaf young people?

Keep praying. Don't give up. Show the world what you can do. God will help you.

Future Fighter for Justice

Indrani

**Pitman,
New Jersey
Model Secondary
School for the Deaf
Washington, D.C.
Class of 1989**

My goal is to work in the legal profession. I would like to be a criminal lawyer," said Indrani Hewsen, a junior at the Model Secondary School for the Deaf (MSSD), in Washington, D.C. "I want to see that justice is done in our world."

Indrani is already working to achieve her goal. She is on the Judicial Board at MSSD and, next year, she will serve as an alternate officer.

"The experience has helped me," she said. "I have developed self-confidence and learned to be assertive on important issues."

Indrani enjoys camping, too, and likes to help others enjoy the experience. One summer, she was a counselor-in-training and volunteer worker at Camp Sun 'n' Fun Kinder Camp. The next summer she worked as a junior counselor at Shadybrook Language and Learning Center.

"I planned activities for the children," she remembered. "I helped feed them and dress them and taught them to care for themselves. I helped them learn proper behavior, too."

Working outside in the summer heat, Indrani brought patience and perseverance to her work.

Indrani is interested in sports. She played right- and left-wing defense on the soccer team of her junior high school in Stamford, Connecticut. The team received statewide recognition two years in a row. Indrani and her teammates won two trophies at the awards banquet. She also won an award for participating on the track team in junior high school.

Driver's Education was her favorite subject last year.

"With my driver's license, I can help my family run errands," she said.

"I love to read, listen to music, and talk with friends," said Indrani, who was recently MSSD student of the month.

Indrani said that she would like to encourage other deaf students to believe in themselves.

"Do what is right for you," she said. "This will inspire others."

South

AIMEE TUCKER

JAMES ADAMS

CHRIS COWDEN

MATT TUXBURY

PAUL SWADLEY

C.E. PRINCE

SHELLIE ABERNATHY

JAIME PRESLEY

DONNA SCOTT

EDDIE HANNA

JON CLEMENTS

Dad's Little Ball Player Becomes Sport Champion

Aimee

**Fort Polk,
Louisiana
Kansas School for
the Deaf
Olathe, Kansas
Class of 1987**

Aimee Tucker's father taught her to play basketball—and that began his daughter's career as a deaf sports star.

A varsity volleyball player from the Kansas School for the Deaf (KSD), Aimee was a Central States Schools for the Deaf (CSSD) all-star for four years. She was team captain during her senior year and was honored by the National Association of the Deaf as a member of the Deaf All-American Volleyball Team. Aimee played in the World Games for the Deaf as a member of the American volleyball team.

Aimee's favorite sport is basketball, although she likes all sports. She was captain of the KSD basketball team for two years and played point guard. She made the CSSD, the Midwest States Schools for the Deaf, and the Two Trails League all-star teams four years in a row. A Deaf All-American player, during one game Aimee scored more than half of her team's points—32 out of 61.

"For a while I wasn't confident," Aimee said. "Now I'm confident of my ability to play and to shoot the ball."

Aimee's mother is a cross-stitch expert and Aimee is learning to do many creative stitches from her.

"I want to show my cross-stitch projects and my sports scrapbook to my children," she said.

Active in school leadership, Aimee was the sophomore representative to the Student Body Council at KSD and chairperson for KSD homecoming. She was also secretary of her freshman class and treasurer of her senior class.

As vice president of the Jayhawk Club, Aimee helped the girls in the dorm have fun together. As vice president of the Dormitory Council, she helped improve dorm rules and planned activities.

Aimee also served first as treasurer, then as secretary, and finally as president of her local Junior National Association of the Deaf (Jr. NAD) chapter. In 1986, she attended the Jr. NAD national convention.

"At the national convention, we attended

workshops. We learned how we could help—and be helped by—the National Association of the Deaf. In other workshops we learned about politics, parliamentary procedure, and Deaf culture," she said.

Aimee entered the Miss Jr. NAD Pageant and won the Miss Congeniality award.

"I was both surprised and proud," she said.

Math is her favorite subject, and Aimee hopes to have a career in accounting. She already has some work experience. She worked as a bookkeeper and file clerk at a city social service agency. She also worked as a file clerk at the civilian personnel office in Fort Leavenworth, Kansas.

Aimee's father is in the army and they have moved often. Her family has also traveled many places in the United States.

"My favorite place is Yellowstone, Wyoming," she said. "The land is beautiful, and we saw geysers and many animals. We had a great time there."

Aimee was born in West Germany, and some day she hopes to travel there and see

For a while I wasn't confident. Now I'm confident of my ability to play and to shoot the ball."

that country again.

"I would like to encourage other deaf students to set goals and then work to attain them," she said. "Be strong and respect people who care for you."

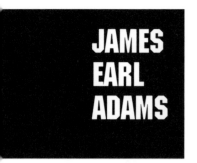

Optimist Award Winner Enjoys Acting

James

**Memphis,
Tennessee
White Station
High School
Memphis,
Tennessee
Class of 1991**

I love to perform. I'm a member of the Deaf Drama Club at White Station High School where I am a junior. When we perform for hearing audiences, they are surprised that deaf people can act just as well as hearing people. We have some hearing people in our club, but the numbers are limited. The club has performed at churches, schools, and community activities, such as Memphis in May. We put on two performances at the Second Baptist Church — one for the adults and another for the youth group. It's fun to travel all around the Memphis area to perform!

I'm the president of the Deaf Drama Club. This responsibility helps me develop my leadership skills. I've been in the club for three years now. Acting helps me develop my confidence — and my physical coordination, too. Some of the deaf students are embarrassed to be in the drama club, but I encourage my friends to join. We show hearing people that we can do the same things that they can. I was voted Best Actor, which makes me feel proud of myself.

In school, I'm on the honor roll. My favorite class is math because I like to learn how to deal with money. I'm also taking English, Spanish, personal computers, acting, and resource. I'm on the basketball team and the track team, too.

During the summer I'm a camp counselor at Dae Valley Camp. Supervising the children is fun, but hard work. During the school year, I always volunteer to help with the Special Olympics. These games are held at my school and are for special-needs students from all over the city. I helped with the Special Olympics in the basketball competition this year.

I won the Optimist Club Award this year for my speech, "The Dream Is Alive." In my speech I said, "My dream in life is to obtain a good education." I will be the first person from my family to go to college. I plan to attend Gallaudet University. Eventually, I would like to get an advanced degree in job counseling or law.

Basically, my interest is in helping people who don't have an education or a job. Most of the time, people who don't have a high school diploma don't get good jobs. Some people don't work at all and just collect money from the government. Others are sad because they are poor and don't have a job. When people get a job, they feel better about themselves. I want to help people to develop a sense of pride and to take care of themselves. Not just deaf people, but all people.

Drugs and alcohol are a big problem in our society. When I marry and have kids, I will teach them about the dangers of drugs — about babies born addicted to crack and about others whose lives have been destroyed by drugs. This is very important.

I go to the Thrifthaven Baptist Church and participate in the youth group. I believe in God, who watches over all of us. I know that God will help me to be honest and to stay away from evil influences.

Some of my family lives in Arkansas and some in Michigan. I have visited both places. I've also been to New Mexico.

The deaf students at White Station High School earned money by having car washes and selling T-shirts. We used this money, along with some donated funds, for several trips. We went to Washington, D.C. On the way, we stopped in Charlottesville, Virginia, to tour Monticello, the home of Thomas Jefferson. In Washington, we visited Gallaudet University, the museums, and several monuments. We toured the White House, the Bureau of Engraving and Printing, and the Capitol. We also met our senator from Tennessee. On another school trip to Florida, we toured Disney World, Epcot Center, and the Kennedy Space Center.

I believe that all people can reach their goals. Nothing is going to prevent me from reaching my goals for I believe strongly in myself and in my ability to do what I set out to do. You can do it, too!

Basically, my interest is in helping people who don't have an education or a job....I want to help people to develop a sense of pride and to take care of themselves. Not just deaf people, but all people."

CHRISTOPHER DALE COWDEN

From Space Travel to Shakespeare, Student Loves Learning

Chris

**Nashville,
Tennessee
Wright Middle
School
Nashville,
Tennessee
Class of 1992**

C hris Cowden, an advanced student in Wright Middle School, in Nashville, Tennessee, enjoys learning about Shakespeare, poetry, space travel, and the United States Constitution. Here is an interview with Chris.

What is your favorite subject in school?

My favorite subject in school is called Excel/ Encore, a special class for students who want to strive for excellence in their schoolwork.

What kind of work have you done in your Excel class?

Last year, we studied Shakespeare's poems, space travel, and the U.S. Constitution, including the Bill of Rights. We read Shakespeare's play *Hamlet*, too.

Do you enjoy it?

Yes. *Hamlet* was easy to read. But the unit on the Constitution and the Bill of Rights was very difficult. Some of the students decided not to participate in the other advanced-placement course, Encore.

Did you participate in Encore?

Oh, yes! I studied African music, the elderly, architecture, and philosophy.

What are your hobbies?

My favorite hobby is reading, especially novels. I also like to read autobiographies and biographies. Now I am reading about famous people like the ballerina Anna Pavlova, the stage actress Sarah Bernhardt, and the famous designer, Coco Chanel. I have read so many books that I just don't know which ones are my favorites. I think Barbara Taylor Bradford and Danielle Steel are good authors.

Do you participate in extracurricular activities?

I am a member of the school newspaper staff. I enjoy writing stories, typing stories into the computer, and selling papers.

Have you won any awards?

Last year I received the Presidential Academic Fitness Award for good citizenship

and good grades. The principal selected the award winners in our school and he sent our names to Washington, D.C. Then, we each received a medal and a plaque with the President's signature on it.

What would you like to do in the future?

Someday, I would like to travel around the world. I've been interested in history since I was very young, and I enjoy learning about the differences between the United States and other countries. I have a Japanese pen pal, so that is one reason why I like to study different cultures. I would also like to visit a country with a primitive culture.

Do you have any advice for other deaf students?

It's fun to learn new information—from classes, TV, newspapers, magazines, and other people. I challenge students to learn something new every day.

Someday, I would like to travel around the world. I've been interested in history since I was very young, and I enjoy learning about the differences between the United States and other countries."

Setting Personal Goals and Keeping Spirits High

Matt

**Oak Ridge,
Tennessee
Oak Ridge High
School
Oak Ridge,
Tennessee
Class of 1986**

Matt Tuxbury, from Oak Ridge, Tennessee, played so many positions in so many sports that once, in the middle of a basketball game, he tucked the ball under his arm as if it were a football and ran down the court trying to make a touchdown.

"Suddenly I realized what I was doing," Matt remembered. "So I stopped and threw the ball to the referee. It was both funny and embarrassing."

A member of the Fellowship of Christian Athletes (FCA), Matt played forward, guard, and center on the Harrison-Chilhowee Baptist Academy basketball team and served as captain for two years. He also played guard, tackle, nose guard, defensive end, and linebacker on his school's football team and earned a letter. When he transferred to Oak Ridge High School, Matt played on his new school's team. Matt also lettered in track and once threw a shot put 38 feet.

"I set personal goals as an athlete and worked hard to achieve them," said Matt.

"Even if we were losing, I tried to keep a positive attitude. I tried to keep my team's spirits high and encourage my teammates to play up to their potential."

Matt credits his religion with helping him keep up his own spirits and fulfill his potential.

"I want to emphasize how important a personal relationship with Christ is for me," he said.

Matt was a member of his school's ministerial club at Harrison-Chilhowee Baptist Academy.

"The purpose of the club was to encourage young people to participate in the church, by speaking, directing music, and teaching Sunday School classes. Our favorite leisure time activity was going to a restaurant to eat together," said Matt.

Matt is involved in two churches, St. Stephen's Episcopal Church and Temple Baptist Church. His parents attend St. Stephen's Episcopal and Matt has served as an acolyte, helping the priest with the communion service. At Temple Baptist

Church, a deaf pastor helps Matt and other deaf people understand the Bible.

"I really enjoy the fellowship I have with other deaf people in church," said Matt.

At school, Matt was secretary and treasurer of the art club. He helped to prepare the school art display during homecoming week.

"I especially enjoyed working on craft projects," said Matt.

At Oak Ridge High School, Matt was the only deaf student in the school during his junior and senior years. Each day, his English teacher encouraged him to take some class time and teach the other students sign language.

"My teacher said that sign language was helpful," he said. "Some of the students had been confused about parts of speech, and learning the signs helped clarify this for them."

At Oak Ridge High, Matt earned a certificate from the Tennessee Board of Vocational Education for being the best cook in his class.

In the summer of 1988, Matt worked for Martin Marietta Energy Systems doing computer drafting and programming. In the fall, he plans to attend Roane State Community College where he will finish his associate's degree in computer science. Then he wants to go to the University of Tennessee and study computer science or business.

Matt hopes to get married, have children, and work full-time for Martin Marietta. He also aspires to elective office. He would run as a Republican, and his eye is on the county court clerkship in Anderson County.

"Study hard, work hard, and don't use drugs and alcohol," Matt advises other deaf students.

Each day, his English teacher encouraged him to take some class time and teach the other students sign language.

Student Writes to Make Dream Come True

Paul

**Toano, Virginia
Lafayette High
School
Williamsburg,
Virginia
Class of 1987**

A reporter and editor for his award-winning school newspaper and author of several published short stories, Paul Swadley graduated from Lafayette High School, in Williamsburg, Virginia. Paul is well on his way to the career of his dreams—in journalism.

Paul was one of the few students accepted in the Young Writers' Workshop at the University of Virginia, an intensive two-week session with journalists and authors. His short story, "The Grey Captain," was runner-up in a scholarship contest.

Paul works hard on his writing. One of his most recent stories, which has an emphasis on conservation, is in its second revision and is being critiqued by friends and instructors from the Young Writers' Workshop.

In high school, Paul was a swimmer. Every morning, he practiced from 5:30 a.m. until 7:00 a.m. with the rest of his teammates. He swam in the 50-meter freestyle, 100-meter breaststroke, 100-meter backstroke, and, occasionally, the 400-meter freestyle. When the swim season was over, Paul and his teammates were district champions.

Paul's family moved to Williamsburg when he was a freshman in high school. Up until that time, his classroom teachers had used cued speech. But in high school, his teachers could not learn a new system of communication to accommodate one deaf student.

"At first I had to depend on hearing peers to help me," Paul said. "But toward the end of my freshman year, I got a cued-speech interpreter for three of my classes. In my junior and senior years, all my classes were interpreted. At William and Mary College, I have a cued-speech interpreter, too."

During the fall of his senior year in high school, Paul worked in Jamestown Festival Park as part of an internship for his history class. Visitors come to the park to see where some of America's first English settlers arrived and what their lives were like.

"Each day, three boats arrived in the harbor to dramatize the settler's arrival," Paul explained. "I wore authentic costumes as I worked in the Indian village or the settler's fort."

"One day, we killed and cooked a pig," he continued. "Another day, we tanned the hide of a deer the way they did it in the seventeenth century. I also served as a cabinetmaker's apprentice and explained the art of cabinetmaking to visitors."

Using his writing talents, Paul also helped write news releases for the historic park.

Now a student at the College of William and Mary, Paul is working part-time as a typist and proofreader for the *Virginia Gazette*, his town's local newspaper. He also began working as a reporter for his college newspaper *The Flat Hat*.

Paul has found time for other college involvements besides writing. He joined the Sigma Alpha Epsilon Fraternity. He played on the fraternity's volleyball and soccer teams and joined the swim team. Overall, his fraternity placed third in the intramural roster.

A member of a triathalon team, Paul

Paul was one of the few students accepted in the Young Writers' Workshop at the University of Virginia, an intensive two-week session with journalists and authors.

does the swimming, while two of his friends handle the cycling and running. He lifts weights, too.

Paul also plans to join the Young Democrats Club for college-age Democrats. "The organization provides a forum in which to debate political issues in local, state, and national government," he said.

He looks forward to a year of study abroad, in either France, Great Britain, or Australia, during his junior year. He plans to travel to France in the summer to visit a friend.

Paul's future goals include going to graduate school to get a master's degree in journalism or government.

"Hopefully, I will be able to achieve my dream of becoming a newspaper editor," he said.

CHARLES EDWARD PRINCE

"Trekkie" Pulls 4.0 at Graduation

C.E.
**Bossier City,
Louisiana
Airline High School
Bossier City,
Louisiana
Class of 1988**

Charles Edward Prince, who lives in Bossier City, Louisiana, graduated from Airline High School with a perfect 4.0 average. A member of the Beta Club, the National Honor Society, the Distributive Education Club of America, and the Chess Club, the boy who calls himself "C.E." helped in after-school activities, too. He was equipment manager for the Airline High School Band, hauling the large musical instruments to and from performances. He also passed out and collected the music. The band director told the reporter for the school newspaper that C.E. was a major asset.

"During the football games, I helped the band set up for halftime performances," he said. "I enjoyed going to all the games and cheering for our school team."

For fun, C.E., an ardent Trekkie, watches reruns of the TV science-fiction show "Star Trek." Of course, he collects "Star Trek" memorabilia. C.E. watches so many "Star Trek" episodes that he has earned the

nickname "Spock," after the character from Vulcan. He has made his own version of "Star Trek," a movielike program that he put on his computer.

C.E. goes to Broadmoor Assembly of God church where he is active in the deaf ministry. C.E. is now in the process of studying to be a lieutenant in the Royal Rangers of the Assembly of God.

"Deaf people need religion because they are sometimes lonely or depressed," said C.E. "Jesus can help. I would like to reach deaf people for Christ."

C.E. sees himself growing stronger in the Lord. He wants to share his favorite Bible verse with other deaf teenagers: *For God so loved the world, that he gave his only begotten Son, that whosoever believeth in Him should not perish, but have everlasting life. (John 3:16)*

C.E.'s biggest earthly love is computers. Since he graduated from high school, C.E. has worked full-time for Softdisk Publishing. He enjoys his job, and he is taking advantage of the many opportunities for

Deaf people need religion beause they are sometimes lonely or depressed. Jesus can help. I would like to reach deaf people for Christ."

advancement that the company offers. He is really interested in brainteasers and strategy games for computers. C.E. hopes to get some of his own computer programs published someday. C.E. wants to continue working with computers and perhaps start his own business.

"My dream is that every home will have a computer in the future," said C.E.

Spotlighted in his school newspaper, C.E. was asked his philosophy of life.

"To have a friend," said C.E., "be a friend. That's success!"

MICHELLE DAWN RICHARDSON ABERNATHY

Communicating through Words, Signs, and Art

Shellie

**McKenney, Virginia
Prince George High School
Prince George, Virginia
Class of 1989**

By the time she was a sophomore, Shellie Abernathy, a student at Prince George High in Prince George, Virginia, had learned more than most people about love and loss.

Shellie was adopted when she was one year old. Her adoptive parents were "really great," she said. "They communicated with me, and they helped me in so many ways."

Shellie and her adopted mother were very close. In 1986, Shellie's adoptive mother died.

"She was my best friend," said Shellie. "I will always remember the wonderful times we had together."

Shellie's school honored her mother by giving sign language books to the library and putting her mother's picture in the front of each book.

Her birth mother lives in California with Shellie's brother.

"I love them, too," Shellie said.

Shellie is very active in her school and in her community. She goes to a class at her church where she helps the members who want to learn how to sign.

"I enjoy my church activities," she said. "I have played on the baseball team for two years. I attend Bible classes with the high school students and young adults."

Shellie wrote "Garfield's ABCs" and won second place in a young authors'contest.

"I was very excited to receive this award," she said.

She is a member of her school's sign language club, where more than 20 students gather to help those who hear learn signs so they can communicate with deaf people. She is also a member of the computer club.

As a sophomore, Shellie made the honor roll during the fourth reporting period.

"Art is my favorite subject," she said. "I enjoy drawing with pencils and painting with watercolors. I like to draw cartoons, too."

Shellie visited Gallaudet University during the student strike for a Deaf President Now.

"I really enjoyed my visit," she said.
Shellie wants to marry a deaf man and
ve several children.

"I hope I will have a happy marriage," she
id. "I don't ever want to divorce."

Shellie wants to study drafting and use
r skills in a business
reer. She also wants
travel and perhaps
e in other states and
untries. Whatever
e does, she does
e best she can!

Shellie is very active in her community. She goes to a class at her church where she helps the members who want to learn how to sign.

Living to the Fullest

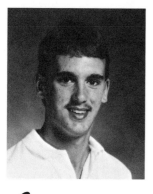

Jaime
**Gastonia, North
Carolina
Ashbrook High
School
Gastonia, North
Carolina
Class of 1989**

I'm an average teenage boy. I like sports, cars, and girls. I like school, but I like summer vacation better.

I became a page for the lawmakers in the North Carolina General Assembly. I took the job just to please my mother, but it turned out to be a terrific experience! I learned a lot and it was so much fun. I met interesting people and saw how state government really works. I worked for Senator Marshall Rauch. Senator Ollie Harris gave me a ride back home after the session ended.

Two years in a row I received certificates for academic achievement at my school's academic awards banquet. I was one of the students selected to attend a conference at Peace College in Raleigh, North Carolina, the state capital. We studied state government and visited the state legislature.

I've always made good grades in school. I have concerned parents and good teachers. During a nine-week period in my sophomore year, I had a 100 average in biology. My science project that year won

first place in both the school and county science fairs.

I like to draw and create pictures, and a a sophomore my favorite subject was art. As a junior, I started to get interested in drafting, and now it is my favorite subject. My instructor asked me to take advanced drafting, a course that most students have to apply for. My instructor told me that I have talent and he thinks I should pursue drafting in college and go into engineering or architecture for my career.

Since second grade, I've played sports. I started by playing T-ball and soccer. Then I developed an interest in BMX bike racing. I've won lots of trophies for BMX bike racing, including one trophy from a national competition held in Charlotte, North Carolina.

After I turned sixteen, I traded my BMX bike for a ten-speed bike. I worked on bike a lot then. Now I work on cars. I am building my own race car and I work on race cars for my stepfather. I hope to compete in a dirt-track race next summer.

34

In junior high I played four sports, but in high school I decided to concentrate on just one—soccer, my favorite. I will never quit playing soccer. I was honored to be able to start on my junior high team in seventh grade and my high school team in tenth grade. I won the most valuable player award my freshman year. I also play on a Class-A select soccer team, and we travel to different cities to play soccer against some of the best athletes in North Carolina. I was one of seven players from Gaston County named to the 1987 Gaston/Cleveland All-Soccer Team.

I enjoy swimming, camping, tubing, and waterskiing. Once, I won first place in the pass, shoot, and dribble competition for the Belmont Abbey College Youth Basketball Teams.

Animals seem to love me—and I love them. Once I brought home a sick, starving kitten and insisted my parents take it to the vet. The kitten needed an operation and, because of my concern, the vet agreed to treat it for a very small charge. Another time, I brought home a chipmunk whose hind legs had been paralyzed by a cat's bite. A friend and I built a cage and took care of that chipmunk for months—until it died.

For a few summers I worked with the Carolina Lawn Service operating a weed eater. Last year, I worked as cleanup person at a local automobile dealership, and this year I have a job with the dealership putting

I have never considered myself handicapped. Deafness doesn't hold me back from people, work, play, sports, or life."

undercoating on cars and trucks.

I hope to get either an academic or athletic scholarship to college. I'm not sure what I want to study, but I'm leaning toward engineering, drafting, or architecture. Whatever I do, I expect to be happy, healthy, and successful. And I expect to have money in my savings account.

I have never considered myself handicapped. Deafness doesn't hold me back from people, work, play, sports, or life. I feel that I am living to the fullest.

My advice to other deaf students is to study hard and get the best education you can. Never be ashamed to ask for help when you need it. You will need it! Everyone does, including hearing people. Turn your deafness into an asset. Most people will go out of their way to help you if you ask. Count your blessings and be grateful for the sharpness of your other senses. Don't ever let deafness keep you from achieving your dreams.

Cheerleader Tackles Books and Aims at Business Career

Donna

Henderson,
North Carolina
Eastern North
Carolina School
for the Deaf
Wilson, North
Carolina
Class of 1991

When Donna Scott, from the Eastern North Carolina School for the Deaf (ENCSD), in Wilson, North Carolina, was in sixth grade, she tried out for the cheerleading squad—and was thrilled when she made it. By the time she was in eighth grade she was the cheerleading squad captain.

"We practice a lot," said Donna. "I was nervous about pep rallies at first, but now I enjoy them."

In addition to cheering, Donna studies a lot. She earned a certificate for most-improved speech and she is on the honor roll. Her favorite subject is science.

"I enjoy studying about frogs, plants, and animals," she said. "I work hard for my teachers."

Donna has learned a lot about history through her school's North Carolina History Club. The club traveled to Washington, D.C. where Donna and the other ENCSD students visited the Capitol, the White House, the Lincoln Memorial, and the Vietnam Memorial. They also visited Gallaudet University and toured the Model Secondary School for the Deaf.

Donna has won prizes for her writing. She wrote a paper on "What the Constitution Means to Me," about the rights of American citizens, and won first place at ENCSD and the right to compete in a county competition and conference. At the county competition, her paper won second place, and Donna was awarded money as a prize.

"My mother, principal, and teachers were proud of me," she said.

Donna lives at the ENCSD dormitory and helps her dorm supervisors in many ways.

"I try to be a good example for the other girls," she said. "I explain the rules to the younger girls and try to keep the dorm clean."

She succeeded, too, because she was awarded a certificate for being the most dependable person in her dorm. Donna was part of a group of exemplary dorm students who went on a special trip to the beach.

In addition to cheering, Donna studies a lot. She earned a certificate for most-improved speech and she is on the honor roll. Her favorite subject is science.

Donna also tries to help her family. She babysits for her cousin, and she taught her cousin to sign and fingerspell.

"I am the only deaf person in my family," Donna said. "My mother is proud because I am mature for my age."

Donna joined her family church when she was thirteen years old and she attends every Sunday. She is a member of the Usher Board and takes part in church programs.

She wants to get married, have children, and be a businesswoman.

THOMAS EDMUND HANNA, JR.

Eddie

**Columbia, South Carolina
A.C. Flora High School
Columbia, South Carolina
Class of 1988**

Working Towards College

Mainstreaming took on a new meaning for Eddie Hanna of Columbia, South Carolina, when he joined seven deaf and thirty hearing teenagers in cleaning up Columbia's parks.

"We all worked well together," said Eddie. "Some of the hearing teenagers learned sign language."

Eddie was glad that the East Columbia Optimist Club stepped forward to employ the teens and pay their salaries. He had filled out fifteen job applications without getting one job offer.

On the park cleanup crew, Eddie and the other teens cleaned, painted, and picked up trash in the morning. Then in the afternoon they had fun. They visited the state capitol and state prison. They also went swimming.

"I appreciate our parks more now," said Eddie. "I was surprised that careless people leave so much trash and write so much graffiti."

Eddie, who was born profoundly deaf, was proud of his deaf co-workers.

"All the deaf students worked hard," he said. "We showed that deaf people can do a good job."

When Eddie was twelve, he went to an antique car show. Soon, he started collecting books and magazines about American cars and trucks. Now he owns a small pickup truck, which he bought himself, called a Mitsubishi Mighty Max.

An active member of the First Baptist Church of Columbia, Eddie enjoys the feeling of community that the other deaf people at his church provide. He joined the Royal Ambassadors, a youth group for boys that studies the Bible and learns about missions.

"I enjoy helping my church," said Eddie. "I work on fund-raising projects. Sometimes, I help in the office or wash the church bus."

Since seventh grade, Eddie has received an award annually for maintaining a high grade-point average. During his senior year, he was inducted into the National Honor Society.

His favorite subjects are government and economics.

"I enjoy learning about laws, the rights of people, and government," said Eddie. "I want to learn how to be a good citizen and consumer."

In his sophomore year, Eddie played defensive end on the football team. In his junior year, he stopped playing football because he wanted to pay attention to his part-time job.

Eddie's job—cleaning, running errands, and stocking items in a convenience store near his home—lasted for one year. In 1987, he was laid off. Very upset, Eddie searched for another job. Instead, he found two.

During the summer, he worked full-time at Columbia's City Hall in the Computer Services Division and on weekends he worked at Huntcliff Townhouse. As a senior, he has all his classes in the morning and can leave school at lunchtime. So Eddie works at Pizza Hut in the afternoons and on weekends.

"I am making big bucks for myself," said

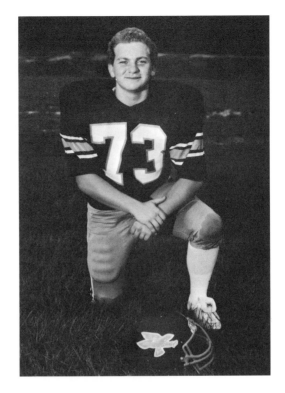

All the deaf students worked hard. We showed that deaf people can do a good job."

Eddie. "And I am saving my money for college."

Accepted by the National Technical Institute for the Deaf (NTID), Eddie plans to major in computer science.

"I visited NTID and I loved it," he said.

In ten years, Eddie hopes to be working as a computer programmer in a large company. He wants to marry a deaf or hard-of-hearing woman, perhaps have some children, and own some antique cars.

"My advice to other deaf students is to study hard, get a good education, get a good job, and stay clean of drugs and alcohol," said Eddie. "Work hard at all you do!"

A Hit on Hearing Sports Teams

Jon
**Grifton, North
Carolina
Eastern North
Carolina School for
the Deaf
Wilson, North
Carolina
Class of 1991**

As a small boy, Jon Clements watched his brother play baseball and longed to join the team. He was accepted, and the coach, realizing he had to work differently with a deaf player, took extra time to help him.

"He saw that I was a person, too," said Jon. "Some people cannot hear with their ears, while other people cannot sign with their hands. We can learn from each other."

"The team really started to work together," Jon said.

They must have worked together superbly because they went on to win first place in the league. Jon, who had wondered if he would be allowed to join the team, was named most valuable player.

Since that time, Jon has played football, soccer, and basketball and has been on the track team at the Eastern North Carolina School for the Deaf (ENCSD). He moved for a short time to Ohio and entered Ellet High School, where he faced a new school full of hearing classmates. His first day of class,

Jon stopped at the gym to shoot some baskets for a few minutes after lunch. As he got ready to leave, the school's athletic director approached him and wanted to know if he could play football.

"I told him I was deaf," said Jon. "And I didn't think I could make the team."

But the athletic director must have felt differently. He introduced Jon to the football coach. A week later, Jon officially tried out for football—and made the first team.

Jon was sorry when his mother got a teaching job in North Carolina.

"I really didn't want to move," he said. "Everyone had been so warm and friendly to me. I told my coach that I had to move, but I really didn't want to."

The team wouldn't let him go without a special farewell.

"Two boys from the football team put a bag over my head and led me to another room. It was a surprise good-bye party for me. The coach gave me a shirt that said 'Ellet Football.'"

Jon learned that his teammates had

never seen a deaf person play football. And that they thought he was one of the best players on the team.

"I was so happy," he said. "I'm proud that I can play as rough as my teammates."

Back at ENCSD, Jon is exploring a wide variety of interests. His favorite subject is math. He enjoys art, painting, woodworking, plumbing and electrical work, animals, sports, photography, and computers.

Jon won first place in an Oratorical Contest sponsored by the Optimist Club. He is also treasurer of his school's history club. As a member of the school's work crew, Jon receives a salary for cleaning classrooms and straightening chairs. During his free time, Jon works with wood. For Christmas, he gave his family gifts that he had made himself.

"I think it's important to be industrious and ambitious," he said. "I like to accept a challenge and take responsibility without being told."

Jon said that he hoped to be able to get a job that would enable him to help people—

Some people cannot hear with their ears, while other people cannot sign with their hands. We can learn from each other."... Jon, who had wondered if he would be allowed to join the team, was named most valuable player.

"not only deaf people, but all people"—in the future.

His advice to others?

"Work hard for what you want," he said. "Don't stand behind and follow. Step out and lead the way!"

Central

BRIAN BIPPUS

LANCE FORSHAY

MARSHA WITTER

TODD HLAVACEK

DEBBIE MULLINS

DEBBIE HUNTER

BETH DONNELLY

CHRIS MAGALSKI

CHRIS SHUE

MATT KRUEGER

KIM BROWN

FAYE STALLWORTH

BRIAN ARNOLD BIPPUS

Playing Center Court for the Third Deaf Generation

Brian

**Anderson, Indiana
Indiana School for
the Deaf
Indianapolis,
Indiana
Class of 1987**

Brian Bippus has more desire and self-discipline than any kid we've ever seen, "Bob Kovatch, varsity basketball coach of the Indiana School for the Deaf (ISD), told a newspaper reporter. "He is the most outstanding player I've ever coached."

Brian's sport *is* basketball. He was the number one rebounder in the entire state of Indiana with an average of 15.4 rebounds per game. He led his city-county division in scoring with an average of 22.8 points per game. He was the first person in ISD's history to make the all-sectional basketball team three years in a row.

Led by Brian, the ISD Orioles had a fantastic year. The team won more games than any other ISD team ever and became the national champions among schools for the deaf.

"Much of our success came from playing as a team," said Brian.

Brian and his teammate, Rocky Murray, have special and long-lasting ties.

"Rocky has been my friend since we

entered ISD together at the age of three," Brian said. "Our mothers, dads, and grandparents were all friends. They met as young students at ISD, too."

"In the 1960s, our dads played together for the Orioles. Our grandfathers both played for the Orioles in the 1930s."

Brian played basketball for the American Athletic Union of the Deaf (AAUD), too. He was among the AAUD players selected to go to the Scarborough/Indianapolis Peace Games in Canada. He is a member of the American basketball team for the 1989 World Games for the Deaf held in New Zealand.

However, basketball is not the only sport in which Brian excels. He played football on the ISD team and was a Deaf All-American defensive back for two years, as well as playing quarterback for the team. Also a baseball player, Brian was a Deaf All-American shortstop.

Brian's leadership ability displayed itself off the playing field as well. Brian was senior class president and sergeant-at-

44

Rocky has been my friend since we entered ISD together at the age of three. Our mothers, dads, and grandparents were all friends. They met as young students at ISD, too."

arms for the Junior National Association of the Deaf. In his college preparatory classes at ISD, Brian earned a 3.6 grade-point average. He graduated third in his class.

"I've always believed in hard work and determination," said Brian. "Go for the best and play hard to win."

The young athlete, scholar, and student leader has set his goals high. His future includes attending Gallaudet University.

"I would like to coach a college or professional basketball team," said Brian. "And I would like to become the first deaf pro basketball player in the United States."

Valedictorian and Eagle Scout Leads in Sports, Student Activities, Too

Lance

**Wichita, Kansas
Kansas School for
the Deaf
Olathe, Kansas
Class of 1987**

Valedictorian of his class at Kansas School for the Deaf (KSD), Lance Forshay earned high marks on all fronts. He achieved top recognition in math and English, and earned the Army Reserve Award for the best academic and athletic ability. He was a member of the Student Body Council, active in the Junior National Association of the Deaf (Jr. NAD), and captain of the KSD football and track teams.

Lance achieved the rank of Eagle Scout, with fifty-four merit badges to his credit.

"The Boy Scouts helped me develop my leadership and outdoor survival skills," said Lance, who served as Quartermaster and Senior Patrol Leader.

Lance won the Optimist Oratorical Scholarship by winning the state Optimist Oratorical Contest. He was one of four KSD students chosen to represent Kansas in the regional contest.

"I enjoy expressing my ideas," said Lance. "I like to tell individuals what I'm thinking, and I enjoy the challenge of speaking in front of a large audience."

All of the speeches at the contest were entitled "Promise Yourself," and Lance talked about the importance of education and discipline.

Lance is involved in his church, too. He serves as Deaf Worship Service Coordinator for the Church of Christ and assists in leading the worship services. He also teaches Sunday School classes. Each summer, Lance attends the National Workshop of Christian Workers for the Deaf. At this important event, church members and pastors throughout the nation meet together for a week.

Lance took advanced math courses throughout high school and achieved high scores on the math portion of the Stanford Achievement Test. Consequently, he won the Maddox Mathematics Award twice for being the best math student at KSD.

"From the time I was very young, I loved mathematics," he said. "I have the ability to understand difficult problems."

He also did well in English and science. Competing against hearing students in the League English Exam Contest, Lance placed fourth. He received the National Academy Achievement Award for science in the spring of 1986.

Lance was vice president of the Student Body Council and active in other leadership organizations, too. He was president, vice president, and treasurer of his class. He helped organize fund-raising—through an auction, clothing sale, stationery sale, and garage sale—to finance the senior class trip to the Bahamas.

In the Jr. NAD, Lance enthusiastically sold golden coupon books and badges to celebrate the 125th anniversary of KSD. He was president of the Student Dorm Council and received the trophy for best behavior in the dorm. Lance also served as president, secretary, and treasurer of the Wildcat Club, a KSD club that helps students develop social and leadership skills.

"We raised money to sponsor events," said Lance. "We earned money for our vacation trip to St. Louis."

He was successful in sports. During his senior year, Lance captained the track team. He won first- and third-place medals for the discus throw, and participated in the javelin throwing events. He was captain of the football team during his senior year. Playing the positions of center and lineman, he received the *K* letter and the all-league award of honorable mention.

Somehow, Lance found time to work part-time in the summer. He cooked, cleaned tables, and worked for Hardee's and Napoleon's restaurants. He also worked as a packer and stock clerk at a food store.

Lance was one of ten winners of a National Fraternal Society of the Deaf Scholarship. As valedictorian of his class, he also earned many more scholarships, including the Staley Roth Scholarship, Southwest College Scholarship, and Kansas Association of the Deaf Scholarship.

"My goal is to major in engineering in college," said Lance, who has been accepted by Gallaudet University.

"Gallaudet has offered me a good engineering program," said Lance. "During the first two years, I will take liberal arts courses. Then, I will focus on engineering classes through a consortium program. This will prepare me well for a career."

Ten years from now, Lance hopes to have a degree from Gallaudet—either in engineering or math and in education of the hearing impaired.

"I would like to teach at a school for the deaf or at a college that has a program for deaf students," he said. "I'm sure that I will enjoy teaching because I like to share my knowledge and beliefs with others."

Lance said that he would also like to have a family and live in a community with a large deaf population. He also hopes that the community is located in a warm climate in the southern part of the United States.

How would Lance encourage others?

"We should desire more challenges in life," he said. "Be patient in moments of difficulty, and listen to what God wants for our lives."

From the time I was very young, I loved mathematics. I have the ability to understand difficult problems."

MARSHA ELLEN WITTER

Deaf Parents Encourage Daughter to Excel

Marsha

**Columbus, Ohio
Upper Arlington
High School
Columbus, Ohio
Class of 1987**

For Marsha Witter the key word is "willpower." "Nothing comes easily," said Marsha. "We have to go out and seize the opportunity."

Marsha knows what she is talking about. With a 3.4 grade-point average, a long list of extracurricular activities, and a coveted listing among the Outstanding College Students of America for 1988, her achievements testify to her determination.

A graduate of Upper Arlington High School in Columbus, Ohio, Marsha describes herself as a hearing-impaired student who wanted to get good grades and was willing to put forth the extra effort to do so.

"At times, it was necessary for me to do additional reading and allow extra study time prior to tests," she said. "I also made copies of class notes—from other students or from the teachers."

The extra work paid off.

The *Arlingtonian,* her school magazine, quoted her algebra teacher as saying "Marsha has the ability to tackle anything. She works twice as hard as anyone else and is very positive."

Marsha credits her parents for helping her, with their love and support—and good example.

"They know what I am going through," she said. "My parents are both deaf, too! They both graduated from college and they never let their deafness interfere with what they want to accomplish."

Marsha said that her participation in clubs and sports has helped her make friends and enjoy school more. She was on the gymnastics team for six years and lettered four out of six of those years. She also lettered two years in softball.

"Softball and gymnastics are very different sports," she noted. "In softball, there is a strong team effort. When we win a game, the feeling of glory can be seen in every individual on the team, and when we lose, disappointment is on every team member's face. In contrast, each person on the gymnastics team has to do her best to beat her teammates as well as her opponent. The pressure on a gymnast is more obvious."

Marsha joined other clubs, too. In the International Club of her high school, she had the chance to meet foreign students and learn about different cultures. She was also a member of the Junior Women's Club and Senior Women's Club.

Marsha was a member of the drill team for two years in high school. Then, during her junior year, she earned one of the three coveted majorette positions with the Upper Arlington High School Marching Band. She continued to "lead the band" throughout her senior year.

"I loved every minute of it," she recalled.

Marsha has visited all the eastern states and many of the western ones. Florida is her favorite vacation spot. Marsha spent 12 days in the Hawaiian Islands with her parents and boyfriend.

"It was a dream come true," Marsha said. "The Hawaiians' slogan is 'Hang loose' and their lifestyle is carefree. They live longer than most of us because of the warm environment and relaxed pace. It was a unique and exciting visit."

After high school graduation, Marsha took a summer job as a clerk. Seeing it as an opportunity to "earn money and make new friends," Marsha typed letters, posted payments on the computer, and helped the secretaries with their work.

But Marsha's greatest experience was her first year at Muskingum College.

"I was the only hearing-impaired student in the whole college," she said. "I got involved in everything that I could fit into my schedule."

She joined a sorority, Chi Alpha Nu, and became a photographer for the school yearbook and newspaper. She was also selected to write for the newspaper. And Marsha managed to work at least seven hours a week for the college public relations department as a photographer and dark-room technician.

Her reward was an academic scholarship and a listing among the Outstanding College Students of America for 1988.

After she graduates from college, Marsha wants to get a job as an accountant and become a Certified Public Accountant (CPA). After she passes the CPA examination—and no one doubts that she will—Marsha wants to start an accounting firm for hearing-impaired clients. She would also like to own a business that sells devices such as clocks, flashing lights, TDDs, and bed vibrators to hearing-impaired people.

Of course, "when the time is right," she wants to marry and have a family.

If her goals seem varied and broad, it is not by accident.

"Life has taught me not to limit myself," she said. "So my advice to deaf young people is to explore freely before making any major decisions. It doesn't matter what kind of impairment a person has. You can do as well as others—if you are willing to put forth the extra work to get good results."

My parents are both deaf, too! They both graduated from college and they never let their deafness interfere with what they want to accomplish."

49

TODD HENRY ROBERT HLAVACEK

Making the Impossible Possible

Todd

**St. Charles, Illinois
Model Secondary
School for the Deaf
Washington, D.C.
Class of 1987**

Todd Hlavacek, a student at the Model Secondary School for the Deaf (MSSD) in Washington, D.C., won first place in the poetry category at the International Creative Arts Festival sponsored by the Center on Deafness for his poem, "The Game."

The Game

Around the green field
With white stripes and figures
I see faces everywhere
Napkins around their necks
Clutching forks and knives
Two carving forks on opposite sides
Steak hopping from one end to another
Salt and Pepper kicking,
Pushing each other for the sirloin
Hut..one..two..hut..hut!
Salt quarterback's fading,
Throwing the steak to the end zone
Fans jumping,
Throwing hands in the air
TOUCHDOWN!!
Pepper players drop their heads
Salt is shaking pepper
The seconds ticking away
The warmth of the steak
0:00!!
The meat is cold!!
Salt has won.

"You can make the impossible possible with your determination and effort," said Todd, quoting his friend Debbie Wright.

And he does. Todd is a peer advisor, member of the Dean's Advisory Board, and member of the Judicial Board at MSSD. He also supervises other students in the dorm. As treasurer of his senior class, Todd is involved in class fund-raising activities—working in the snack bar and helping with Sunday afternoon car washes—as well as collecting aluminum cans as a community service project.

Todd has received awards for his service. He received the Most Promising Paralegal Award and the Judicial Coordinator's Award for his work on the Judicial Board. He also received the National Leadership Merit Award and the National Leadership and Service Award. Todd earned a place in the Gallaudet Young Scholars Program—twice.

"The first year of the Young Scholars Program, we studied the sun and sunspots," said Todd. "We also applied some

50

physics and calculus in doing solar experiments. During the second year, we studied the mechanics of physics."

Calculus, physics, and mechanics come easily to Todd because mathematics is his favorite subject.

"I enjoy playing with numbers," he said.

Todd is mainstreamed into a nearby public school precalculus and statistics class, and hopes to go to college and major in engineering. Todd received the National Mathematics Award and the All-American Achievement Award.

Todd plays sports, too. He won a Deaf All-American Honorable Mention from the National Association of the Deaf for his contributions as sweeper and center fullback on MSSD's varsity soccer team.

He was also named Athlete of the Month this year for his contribution to the MSSD baseball team. With Todd playing shortstop, second base, right field, and acting as a pinch-runner, the MSSD team won second place in the play-offs for the first time in its history.

Todd plays on the intramural teams, too, including softball, basketball, football, and blind volleyball. He participated in the Intramural Air Hockey Tourney. As co-chair of the sports banquet, Todd oversaw the committee work, got permission to use equipment and facilities, and presented information about absent participants to the audience.

Todd also holds part-time jobs. He cleans, dusts, vacuums, and washes windows with a professional housecleaning service. In the past, he has sorted and delivered the mail that the post office delivers to his school.

"With frustration, persistence, and the support of your friends and family, you will succeed in what you do," said Todd.

Todd is mainstreamed into a nearby public school precalculus and statistics class, and hopes to go to college and major in engineering.

DEBORAH MULLINS

Debbie

**Olathe, Kansas
Kansas School for
the Deaf
Olathe, Kansas
Class of 1987**

"My Responsibility ...Is to Be Involved"

*I*nvolvement is one of the most important responsibilities of citizenship," wrote Debbie Mullins, a senior at the Kansas School for the Deaf (KSD), in a speech for the Optimist Oratorical Contest. "My responsibility as a good citizen is to be involved in government, organizations, and community projects to make our country a better place to live."

Debbie delivered the speech in front of the Optimist Club, using sign language with a voice interpreter. The Optimist Club awarded her a $1,000 scholarship.

Debbie has won other writing awards, too. She won third place in the creative writing (short story) division of the International Creative Arts Festival, sponsored by the Center on Deafness. Her story was entitled "I'll Never Forget Cindy."

A member of the staff of the *Kansas Star*, the KSD newspaper, Debbie has written several stories for publication. Her story about the volleyball team was printed in the *Silent News*, a national news magazine for deaf people.

Debbie also captained both the KSD basketball and volleyball teams for two years. In basketball, she won an honorable mention in the Two Trails League and a place on the all-star team during the Central States Schools for the Deaf (CSSD) tournament. During the tournament, she received a plaque for being the most inspirational player.

Debbie broke the school record in the 400-yard dash, running it in 1:06 minutes. But her favorite sport is volleyball, so she was delighted to be selected for the CSSD all-star volleyball team.

In all, Debbie has won thirty-six medals and a sportsmanship trophy for her participation in school sports. She has won several ribbons for her three years as a member of the cheerleading squad, and she was part of the squad of girls that won first place in cheerleader camp.

Debbie participates in her student government. She served as secretary of the Student Council in her sophomore year and president in her junior year.

"The purpose of the Student Council is to improve relationships between students and teachers," she said. "We also plan school activities and parties—such as homecoming, the Valentine's Day party, winter royalty, and spring prom."

Debbie participated royally in the events she helped plan. Last year, she was chosen as a junior princess at homecoming and then queen for winter royalty. This year, she was homecoming queen and a princess at winter royalty.

She is secretary of her class and vice president of the KSD Junior National Association of the Deaf (Jr. NAD) this year. She attended the Jr. NAD convention in Mississippi, where she participated in a parliamentary procedure workshop, trivia game, mini-carnival, and mock debate.

"I met many people there," she said. "And I learned a lot about leadership."

She traveled to Washington, D.C., to participate in Close-Up, a program for high school students who want to learn more about how the U.S. government operates.

My responsibility as a good citizen is to be involved in government, organizations, and community projects to make our country a better place to live."

Debbie hopes to go to Gallaudet University and to pursue a career in journalism.

"I want to encourage other deaf teenagers to become involved in many activities in order to find out their real interests, always do their best, and set a good example for others," she said.

DEBRA LIANE HUNTER

Student Writes One President and Two Presidents Answer

Debbie

**Columbus, Ohio
Brookhaven
High School
Columbus, Ohio
Class of 1988**

When Debbie Hunter, a student at Brookhaven High in Columbus, Ohio, wrote President Ronald Reagan about captioning the world news, President Reagan wrote her back, and her great-uncle put the letter in his newspaper. Officials from the National Captioning Institute (NCI) saw the letter, were impressed, and invited Debbie to NCI headquarters in Falls Church, Virginia, near Washington, D.C. Debbie traveled there and met the president of NCI.

"I am proud that I wrote to President Reagan," said Debbie. "After that, they put more captioned programs on TV."

Debbie may be getting used to talking with celebrities. In 1984, she met rock star Kenny Rogers backstage after a concert in Cleveland.

"I had a special sticker," she said. "It said 'Kenny Rogers' Special Guest.' A lot of people had a sticker just like it. Gene Roy, the road manager, and I talked first, and he put me first in the line."

"Kenny came out and talked to me. I just could not believe he was really there. He kissed me on the cheek and told me to stay until after he met the other people. Then he autographed a picture I had drawn of him.

"I will never forget that moment. He is my hero. It was a dream come true!" Debbie concluded.

In high school, Debbie was mainstreamed in all her classes, except English and American History. She was on the yearbook staff and a member of the National Honor Society.

She went to Washington, D.C., and spent a week studying the workings of the government with other students in the Close-Up program.

Debbie performed with a synchronized swim team for four years. The only deaf girl on the team, Debbie had to keep time to the music by counting to herself or peeking at her teammates.

"It was hard for me," she said. "But it was a lot of fun. It's like dancing in the water."

Debbie is an artist. She has taken private

art lessons for five years, and won almost fifty ribbons, two trophies, and five Best of Show awards for her work. She has received several awards for her writing, too, including two commendations from the Ohio House of Representatives.

"I enjoy writing stories and poems," she said.

Three years ago, Debbie began training her dog, Cotton, to work as a hearing dog. After a lot of hard work, Cotton learned to alert her to sounds in the home and became a certified hearing dog.

Debbie enjoys taking a vacation every year, too.

"I learn a lot from the places I visit," she said. "My favorite part of a vacation is what I learn from it."

Debbie plans to enter the National Technical Institute for the Deaf at the Rochester Institute of Technology. Her goals are to become a professional artist and author and to make the world a better place for hearing-impaired and other handicapped people.

The only deaf girl on the team, Debbie had to keep time to the music by counting to herself or peeking at her teammates.

"Don't Let Frustration Stop You"

Beth

**Elm Grove,
Wisconsin
Brookfield East
High School
Brookfield,
Wisconsin
Class of 1987**

One of two juniors in her high school who were elected to go to Wisconsin Girls' State, Beth Donnelly calls that time of learning how government works by "doing it," the most exciting experience of her life. She was elected County Clerk of Circuit Court during the week-long gathering held at the University of Wisconsin-Madison.

"I made a lot of great friends and have happy memories," said Beth, who graduated from Brookfield East High School in 1987. "The Badger Girls' State really boosted my confidence so that now I feel very proud of who I am."

Beth is the youngest of six children, four of whom are sisters, who, like herself, have a moderately severe hearing loss.

"We are the first members of either of my parents' families to have this type of high-frequency sensorineural hearing loss," she said.

But she has not let it stop her. All her life, she has been in mainstream programs—through schools in Boston, Massachusetts; Minneapolis, Minnesota; and then Elm Grove, a suburb of Milwaukee, Wisconsin.

In addition to an academic and extra-curricular performance strong enough to ensure her selection to girls' state, Beth participated in various varsity sports, such as basketball, golf, and track. In golf, she was named all-conference.

In her free time, Beth did volunteer work in her community. She began by helping a local food program serve food to needy families in downtown Milwaukee. Then she helped mentally retarded children, assisting in the track and field events of the Special Olympics. She also helped rebuild a home through Habitat for Humanity. Beth now helps provide services for handicapped students at her university.

Despite a busy schedule, Beth Ann pulled a 3.4 grade-point average during her freshman year at Miami University in Oxford, Ohio. She is majoring in fine arts.

She hopes to find work in the art department of a corporation and settle down either in New England or the Midwest.

Beth is the youngest of six children, four of whom are sisters, who, like herself, have a moderately severe hearing loss.

"Life has treated me well," said Beth. "There have been some problems that I have had to face, but I have been able to face most of them and still see the bright side."

She credits her family and friends with giving her the self-confidence to maintain such a positive attitude.

"They continue to love me," she said. "They only pressure me to be the best Beth Donnelly I can be. No matter where I am or what I am doing, I certainly work at that."

Beth understands that accepting a hearing impairment can be hard.

"For those of you who may be experiencing frustrations or having a hard time accepting your hearing loss, I just want to say it's all right to be frustrated," she said.

"I just don't believe in letting frustration stop you. It took me a long time to realize it, but it was worth the wait, because now I fully appreciate the abilities I have. The key is to like yourself first, and think positive thoughts about your abilities."

"Be the best you can be!"

Artist Lines Up Scholarship Money for College

Chris

**Columbus, Ohio
Brookhaven High
School
Columbus, Ohio
Class of 1988**

An accomplished artist, with several Best of Show awards to her credit, Chris Magalski of Brookhaven High School in Columbus, Ohio, is a member of the National Honor Society and active in her church and community organizations.

Here is an interview with Chris.

How did you become involved in art competitions?

I began taking art lessons when I was ten years old. I entered the International Creative Arts Festival in Chicago for the first time when I was twelve, and I earned a third-place ribbon for my oil painting.

Did you ever win Best of Show?

I have won Best of Show three times—1983, 1985, and 1986. In 1987, I won the award for Most Unique.

What medium do you work in and what sorts of subjects do you paint?

I prefer to work in pastels. I did a seascape, a blue jay, and a still life of dried flowers for my Best of Show awards. I won Most Unique with a pastel of rocks and driftwood.

What subjects do you take at school?

I take classes such as chemistry, Latin, and trigonometry to prepare myself for college.

Do you get good grades?

Yes. It is quite a challenge to maintain a high average. I am on the honor roll and I was inducted into the National Honor Society. I have already received two scholarships to the University of Akron—one for art and one for academics.

Are you involved in any extracurricular activities?

I am a member of the yearbook staff and I serve as team statistician for our varsity volleyball team at Brookhaven High. I was also manager and scorekeeper for the intramural team for two years. At my church, I am involved in the teen program.

Are you involved in any deafness-related organizations?

I have been a member of Self-Help for Hard of Hearing (SHHH) for two years. We meet at the public library. SHHH supports deaf people by informing them about jobs and communication devices that are available.

Have you ever held a job?

Oh, yes. My first job was a summer job at the Ohio Department of Aging. I worked on the computer, preparing discount cards for senior citizens.

What are your career plans for the future?

I hope to go to college and become a graphic designer. I want to design graphics on the computer for businesses and the entertainment industry. I also dream of making a videotape, speaking and signing on the tape about my work as a graphic designer, so that other deaf, hard-of-hearing, and hearing people can learn about graphic design.

I *also dream of making a videotape, speaking and signing on the tape about my work as a graphic designer, so that other deaf, hard-of-hearing, and hearing people can learn about graphic design."*

And what about your personal plans?

I'd like to get married, have two children, a big house or condominium with a beautiful backyard, and a white cockatoo as a pet.

How do you feel about your deafness?

My deafness makes me feel special—but not handicapped. I am glad that I function well with hearing people. I enjoy using the special devices for deaf people. They help me be more independent.

Do you have any advice for other deaf students?

Each of us is special. You are special, too. Discover your talents and work to achieve your dreams.

Student Gets Bones Pinned— and Plays On

Chris
Akron, Ohio
Goodyear Middle School
Akron, Ohio
Class of 1991

An honor roll student who coaches Little League baseball, Chris Shue, a student at Goodyear Middle School in Akron, Ohio, starts every day with a dose of insulin. Chris has diabetes, a chronic disease that requires daily monitoring. He also has three steel pins in his left hip to help his bones work together properly.

"When I was younger, I grew very fast, and some of my bones didn't grow fast enough," said Chris.

The pins enable him to play sports. Nothing seems to slow him down. Chris is a trophy-winning fullback for his school's soccer team. He enjoys basketball and golf, and he has a bowling trophy, too. He works out regularly at a nearby health spa. Always one to combine work and play, when Chris started working at McDonald's, he joined their softball team and played outfield.

All this doesn't stop Chris from getting good grades at school. He has made the merit roll five times, with an average of 3.0 or better, and the honor roll, with an average of 4.0, once.

Science and history are Chris's favorite subjects. He won an award in the science fair last year.

"These subjects are easy for me," he said.

A straight-*A* student in algebra, Chris helped to tutor the hearing students in his class.

He was also the junior representative to the Panda Club, a school club dedicated to preventing alcohol and drug abuse.

Chris is involved in two church youth groups—one at Emmanual Baptist Church and another at Park Methodist Church. He goes to classes for hearing-impaired young people at the Baptist church and attends the Methodist church with his mother. In summer, he helps supervise the younger children at Vacation Bible School.

A member of the Boy Scouts, Chris has earned many merit badges. He also has a Red Cross swimming certificate.

For two years, he worked for the Akron Summer Youth Program. He bought a TDD

with the money he made. Now, he has a job at McDonald's, working on the grill.

"When I graduate from high school, I would like to study drafting and commercial art at the National Technical Institute for the Deaf," said Chris, who has already been accepted into drafting and engineering prevocational classes in high school.

"My goal is to become a drafting engineer for a major company. I want to own a Mustang GT convertible, get married, and have a family. Since there have been many recent advances in surgery, I hope to have a cochlear implant, too," said Chris.

His advice to other deaf students is simple.

"Take any opportunity that comes your way," he suggests. "Get all the experience you can. Keep trying. Don't give up!"

My goal is to become a drafting engineer for a major company. I want to own a Mustang GT convertible, get married, and have a family."

MATTHEW GEORGE KRUEGER

High Achievements, Higher Goals

Matt

**Michigan City,
Indiana
Indiana School for
the Deaf
Indianapolis,
Indiana
Class of 1989**

By the time he was a junior, Matt Krueger, a student at the Indiana School for the Deaf (ISD), had chalked up success as a scholar, actor, photographer, and student leader. Ultimately, Matt wants to be the president of Gallaudet University.

In 1985, Matt's achievements in academic and social areas helped him compete against 300 students and become one of the fifteen to enter the Gallaudet Young Scholars Program, a four-week program for gifted hearing-impaired students.

"The theme of the four-week program was solar physics," said Matt. "We went to Gallaudet University, met deaf scientists, and took field trips to the Goddard Space Flight Center, the Smithsonian Institution, and the Naval Observatory."

At the end of the program, the students voted Matt the Most Likely to Succeed, Best Smile, Best Laugh, and Most Positive Attitude. His success was probably part of the reason Matt was able to return to the Young Scholars Program in 1986, to take a four-week course in marine biology.

A member of Wildfire, a sign-singing, dancing, and mime group, Matt traveled throughout Indiana and the Midwest with the group, giving concerts to increase deaf awareness. Every spring, the group competes in the Regional Center on Deafness Performing Arts Contest. In 1984, Matt was named Most Supportive Member.

"I became interested in music and drama by watching my brothers participate in the school band and in plays," Matt stated.

Matt has chalked up photographic achievements, too. He won second place in the photographic category of the International Creative Arts Festival, sponsored by the Center on Deafness. Matt received a personal letter congratulating him on his award from Governor Orr of Indiana.

Involved in the Junior National Association of the Deaf (Jr. NAD), Matt has been vice president and president of the Jr. NAD chapter at ISD. He went to the Jr. NAD national convention in Washington, D.C., in 1986. The following year, he was elected parliamentary procedure advisor.

Matt also won the Byron B. Burnes Leadership Award, enabling him to go to the Jr. NAD Youth Leadership Camp, in Pengilly, Minnesota for four weeks.

Matt served as vice president and then president of ISD's Student Council. He was elected parliamentary advisor during his senior year. As part of the Student Council, he helped to plan school projects, including Teacher Appreciation Day and basketball homecoming weekend.

Matt has been active in his class, too. He served as class treasurer and president. He was responsible for planning the successful Junior Prom, Junior Variety Show, and the senior trip.

When he was a sophomore, Matt was one of six winners of a scholarship to study in Mexico for three weeks.

"It was fantastic!" he said. "It was one of the golden opportunities of a lifetime."

ISD was the first school for deaf students to participate in the program at Cuernavaca, Mexico. Matt and the other students met several deaf Mexicans.

"We learned to communicate with them through gestures very quickly," Matt said.

Matt was one of two deaf boys who joined 1,000 hearing boys and attended Hoosier Boys' State, sponsored by the American Legion. At the conference, Matt won the W. W. Breedlove Outstanding Citizen Award, which entitled him to be

one of the two Indiana boys to attend Boys' Nation.

Matt is grateful to his alma mater.

"I often wonder what I would be like if I had not come to ISD," he said. "I know that I would not be the person that I am now. ISD has provided opportunities for me to achieve in many ways. It is my second home."

Matt hopes to earn scholarships to continue his education. He plans on attaining degrees in administration and teaching.

"I hope to have a position such as principal or superintendent of a school for the deaf," he said. "I hope to be another deaf president of Gallaudet University."

Whatever happens, Matt is certain that his future will be successful.

"I am proud of my accomplishments," he said. "And I enjoy helping others attain their goals, too. Be strong. Be positive. Do your best. And you will succeed."

❚ hope to be another deaf president of Gallaudet University."

ACTRESS ASSUMES LEADERSHIP ROLES

Kim

**Omaha, Nebraska
Omaha Burke
High School
Omaha, Nebraska
Class of 1988**

Kim Brown, a student at Omaha Burke High School in Omaha, Nebraska, has chalked up some impressive and varied successes. Kim is active in community theatre, the Junior National Association of the Deaf (Jr. NAD), Junior Achievement, and her school swim team.

Kim acted in the Omaha Community Playhouse production of *Children of a Lesser God*. The group went to North Platte, Nebraska, for the state competition—and won first place.

"We were so excited," said Kim. "It was the first time that the Omaha Community Playhouse had won first place in the state competition in 25 years."

"Traveling with the community theatre group was a marvelous experience. Most of the actors and actresses in the play were deaf—and acting in this play gave me an opportunity to understand myself better. It also gave me a sense of accomplishment."

So did the summers Kim spent in Boys' Town, participating in the Summer Pro-

gram for Gifted Hearing-Impaired Youth. The program involved a week of camping, three weeks of study in the classroom, and one week of drama with Bernard Bragg, a famous deaf actor. The young people also went hiking and rock climbing.

"At first some of it was scary," said Kim. "But we worked through our anxieties and learned to feel like a family.

Each summer the students studied a different topic and the extra study helped Kim back in the classroom, too. But the best part about the Boys' Town program, according to Kim, was meeting other deaf students.

"I met many outstanding deaf students," Kim said. "And they became such special friends. They encouraged me and advised me. I greatly admire them. They made me realize that I can be successful, too. Deafness should never stop us from achieving our goals."

"Each year, when it was time to go home," Kim stated, "I cried because it was so hard for me to leave."

Back at Omaha Burke High School, Kim remained active with other deaf students. She was elected vice president and then president of the Junior National Association of the Deaf (Jr. NAD), an organization that helps students develop the necessary leadership skills to be of service to the deaf community.

"I was so happy to be elected president," said Kim. "The job gave me practice in decision making, and helped prepare me to fulfill my goal of eventually becoming one of the officers of the National Association of the Deaf."

Kim also was chosen as a delegate to the Jr. NAD convention in Fremont, California. There she was first runner-up in the Miss Jr. NAD Pageant, received the Miss Congeniality award, and was picked to represent the Western Region of the United States at the 39th Biennial Convention of the National Association of the Deaf.

Kim attended the Jr. NAD Midwest Leadership Conference and won an award for serving deaf people in various organizational capacities.

"The speakers at the conference were successful deaf people," she said. "They were very encouraging. I learned that you really have to feel good about yourself before you can try anything risky."

As a sophomore, Kim joined Junior Achievement, an organization for teens who are interested in business. Suddenly, Kim found herself part of the Goodyear Company and a small group of students that wanted to make and sell bookshelves and wooden cutting boards.

"At first I didn't think I could do it," she said. "But I had a partner who was willing to work with me."

At the end of the year, Kim's company had made and sold enough bookshelves and cutting boards to win the Best Company of the Year award.

"Many times in my life, I wanted to attend a residential school for the deaf," Kim said. "I wanted to be part of Deaf culture. Students at residential schools have deaf teachers. They also have better chances to participate in sports and clubs."

But when she reached her senior year in high school, Kim realized that, as a mainstream student, she had some special opportunities, too.

"I like being close to my family," she said. "Also I want to get the same education as hearing students."

Kim plans to go to Gallaudet University and major in psychology. She wants to get a doctoral degree in psychology from California State University in Northridge and become a psychologist who serves deaf clients.

She hopes to travel around the world— perhaps as an NAD board member—to visit programs for deaf people, giving the people themselves help and encouragement.

"Don't just sit around and dream all the time," Kim advises. "You have to work hard and give up some of your fun times. Deafness has nothing to do with success. It's your brain and motivation that count. Go for it!"

The job gave me practice in decision making, and helped prepare me to fulfill my goal of eventually becoming one of the officers of the National Association of the Deaf."

Cheerleader Captain Roots for Computer Career

Faye
**Columbus, Ohio
Brookhaven
High School
Columbus, Ohio
Class of 1988**

Captain of the cheerleaders for the Lone Stars, a semiprofessional football team, Faye Stallworth, a student at Brookhaven High School in Columbus, Ohio, has been leading cheers on many fronts for a long time.

Faye was chosen for the Brookhaven Drill Team, and went to drill camp at Ohio State University. Her team marched in the parade and won second place in the competition. Faye supported the other girls by helping them get dressed and line up in formation.

"It was fun and I made a lot of new friends," said Faye.

A good student who maintains a *B* average, Faye likes her science classes best.

"I'm interested in studying plant and animal life," she said.

In ninth grade, Faye took a home economics course and modeled the shirt she made herself in a fashion show. In eleventh grade she made a jacket and matching pants. People liked her sewing so much that they asked her to make clothes for them.

Faye is also interested in computers. In her junior year, she got a job as a data-entry clerk, entering information about rented and leased cars on a large computer.

"It was a good experience for me," said Faye. "I felt responsible, grown up, and equal to the other adults who worked there."

Faye credits one of her teachers with getting her interested in computers. In the next ten years, she wants to receive a college degree in computer science. Then, she wants to travel. She hopes to write a book about culture, too.

"I would like to have a career in writing, as well as in computer science," said Faye.

Faye looks forward to having her own apartment, with nice furniture and dishes—and a dishwasher. She wants a car, too, so that she and her friends can go shopping together.

"Don't just sit there in your own silent world," Faye advises deaf students. "Get out and meet new people. Learn a skill and find a job. Let others know we deaf people are capable of doing as much as anyone else."

West

Religion Important to Young Achiever

Laura

**Dallas, Texas
W. W. Samuell
High School
Dallas, Texas
Class of 1988**

My goal is to earn a doctoral degree in deaf education, become a successful teacher, and then start my own Christian school. I've wanted to start a Christian school for deaf children since I was nine years old.

All of my life, I have attended the Silent Friends Chapel of the First Baptist Church in Dallas with my parents, who are deaf, too. Last summer, I assisted our Minister of Education at Silent Friends Chapel. This was my first job, and I really enjoyed the opportunity to work at my church. I became Children's Director, a position I will hold until I leave for college.

I have been involved with the youth department of our church for four years. I was department secretary for the Youth Council. We planned a variety of activities for young people, including Bible studies and parties.

Each year, the Baptist General Convention of Texas sponsors a Bible drill and essay competition. During the Bible drill,

all the participants try to find Bible verses quickly. The director says "Attention," and we stand straight. Then he says "Present Bibles," and we use both hands to bring out our Bibles and hold them before us. Then the director gives us a verse from the Bible to find. We have eight seconds to find each verse. When we find it, we move one step forward. The person who steps forward first gets bonus points. In three years, I memorized more than 150 verses.

I was the first deaf person to enter the Texas Youth Bible Drill. The first year, I won first place in the regional drill and went to the state semifinals. The next two years, I made it all the way to the state finals and won third place both years. Then, I represented Texas at the National Bible Drill at Glorieta, New Mexico—and won first place.

In 1986, I won second place in the Youth Essay Competition with an essay called "How to Get More People Involved in Church Training." I am president of the Junior Texas Baptist Conference of the Deaf, secretary of the Teen Baptist Athletic Association of the

Deaf, and secretary of the Junior Southern Baptist Conference of the Deaf. I have written a Christmas and an Easter play and I will lead the deaf choir at the Texas Baptist Conference of the Deaf.

At the W. W. Samuell High School, where 85 deaf students attended school with 1,500 hearing students, I was involved with the Student Council. During my junior year, I was elected class secretary, the first deaf student to be elected. I was re-elected secretary during my senior year.

The year our Junior National Association of the Deaf (Jr. NAD) chapter started at my school, I was secretary. I wrote up information about our new chapter and sent it to the national *Jr. NAD Newsletter,* which published it. The second and third years our chapter existed, I was president. I am also editor-in-chief of *Campus Notes,* a newsletter published by our Jr. NAD Chapter that circulates through all four of the Dallas regional schools for deaf students.

I like my work with the Jr. NAD because I enjoy trying to think of new ideas and new ways of doing things. In the past two years, our chapter has become a student-run organization and our membership has increased from 14 to 32. Almost one-third of the deaf students at our school now belong.

I served as treasurer and then president of the Deaf Pep Club. Many deaf students are involved in the club. We have about five deaf students—including myself—on the cheerleading squad this year. A story about the deaf cheerleaders was in the *Dallas Morning News.*

I was honored to receive a national award from the United States Achievement Academy for my work in history and government and to be inducted into the National Honor Society. I graduated with honors in the top ten percent of my graduating class and received scholarships from the Texas Association of Parents and Educators of the Deaf and from the Dallas School Administrators' Association. I was recognized as one of 150 outstanding graduates of 1988 in the Dallas Independent School District. I was the only deaf outstanding graduate from my school.

My favorite subject during my junior year was accounting. I found it was fun to analyze accounts. I also love to type. During my senior year, my favorite subject was English because we read many interesting stories.

In the next ten years, I hope to finish college with advanced degrees in deaf education. I plan to go to Lamar University in Beaumont, Texas, and become involved in the National Student Speech, Language, and Hearing Association and the Signing Cardinals.

I also hope to marry a wonderful Christian man who will support me in my wide variety of activities—the way my family has through the years. Perseverance and a positive attitude are important. I strongly encourage deaf students to stand up for their rights in whatever they strive to do. Don't be afraid to become involved with hearing people. Be confident.

Perseverance and a positive attitude are important. I strongly encourage deaf students to stand up for their rights in whatever they strive to do. Don't be afraid to become involved with hearing people. Be confident."

New Arrival Finds Old Skills Helpful in Making Friends

Amanda

**Chandler, Arizona
Corona del Sol
High School
Tempe, Arizona
Class of 1989**

Amanda Kaumans was getting ready to enter her junior year in high school when her family moved. As she entered Corona del Sol High School in Tempe, Arizona, Amanda faced adapting to a new home, a new state, a new school, and new friends.

How did you feel entering your new school?

I was a little nervous at first. Corona del Sol is a public school with about 2,000 hearing students and very few deaf students. But I made friends quickly with two deaf girls. Then I made hearing friends, too.

Do you like your school?

I like my school very much. We have interpreters for our classes, and I'm involved in several school clubs. I think it is important to get the most out of every opportunity—going to classes and participating in other school activities.

What are some of the activities?

I was part of the Close-Up program. I traveled to Washington, D.C., with other students from my school to see how the government works. It was a fantastic experience!

What school clubs do you belong to?

I'm a member of Students Against Drunk Driving (SADD). We make posters and signs to encourage students not to drink and drive. Also, I'm involved in the M.I.M.E. Vice Club, a drama club, which is lots of fun and good experience. I'm in the art club, too. Often, I design posters for my drama and speech classes and I have displayed my graphic designs in the Tempe Art Show and in *Spectrum*, our school magazine. I've done layouts for the magazine, too.

What is your favorite subject?

English. I like to write poetry. I really enjoyed forensics class, too. In forensics, I learned to write and give speeches.

Do you play sports?

Yes. I play forward on our intramural basketball team. We won third place this year. And I bowl on my family's bowling team—the Generation Gap. We won the second-place trophy our second year in the league. I have first- and second-place trophies myself, too.

Are you involved in clubs outside of school?

I'm a member of a church teen group. Every Wednesday night we get together and study the Bible. We call our meetings Wednesday Nite Live. We go on outings and play softball with teams from other churches. I'm a member of Young Life, a community organization of teenagers who share what it means to be Christian with other teenagers. We have dramas, guest speakers, and discussions.

What about community service?

I like to be involved in projects that help my community. Last summer, I helped clean the area around our community swimming pool. And I volunteered to serve as a sign language teacher. I am a member of the 4-H club, too, and it has given me the opportunity to develop my art skills. I have won art awards as part of 4-H.

Anything else?

Last year, I worked in the Chandler Public Library. I shelved books, filed cards, and helped students find books and other information. I also worked as an aide in the library and bookstore at my high school.

I think it is important to get the most out of every opportunity—going to classes and participating in other school activities."

What do you see yourself doing ten years from now?

I'll be 27 in 10 years—still young with a promising future. I hope to have a career in commercial art. I would also like to be a counselor at a summer camp and rehabilitation center. I hope to have a comfortable home in the country and raise puppies to serve deaf and blind people.

If you made a lot of money, what would you do with it?

I'd buy a big home for teens who are lost on the streets. I love people, and I want to show love and respect to everyone I meet.

Do you have any words of encouragement for other deaf teens?

Even if it is hard to communicate, feel free to talk to hearing people. Treat each person specially. Your smile will encourage others.

Math Whiz Accepts Challenges

Michael

**Aloha, Oregon
Holy Family
Catholic School
Portland, Oregon
Class of 1992**

"My life has always been hard because I have trouble hearing," said Michael Pollock, a student at Holy Family Catholic School. "I read lips, and I understand what is said most of the time. But sometimes it is hard for me to understand my friends when they are in a group and talking rapidly."

But Michael succeeds in understanding and making himself understood. He tutors the second- and sixth-grade students in math.

"Science and math are my favorite subjects," said Michael.

In seventh grade, Michael was already hard at work on the eighth-grade math book. He is looking forward to taking algebra next year.

"I like researching and discussing new topics," he said. "Science and math activities make learning fun."

Michael was born in California and he started school in Hayward.

"That was wonderful for me," he said. "I made several friends who were hearing-impaired."

In 1979, his family moved to Oregon. At first, Michael went to the regional program for the hearing impaired, riding the bus thirty miles each way to and from school. Michael remembered that it was not a pleasant experience because it was difficult to make friends.

Then he transferred to Tucker-Maxon Oral School.

"The teachers and students at Tucker-Maxon were great influences on me," said Michael. "I made the most progress I have ever made."

In 1984, he entered the fifth grade at Holy Family School, where he was mainstreamed into classes of hearing students.

"The first three months were very difficult for me," he said.

But a resource teacher from Tucker-Maxon came to his new school and worked with Michael for about an hour every day, reviewing the difficult subjects.

"In sixth grade, I learned several ways to improve my work," said Michael. "I learned how to review the examples in

I read lips, and I understand what is said most of the time. But sometimes it is hard for me to understand my friends when they are in a group and talking rapidly."

the book, and if I didn't understand, to ask the teacher to explain."

Perhaps Michael's hard work is paying off. When Dr. Daniel Ling gave a lecture on speech at a convention of the Alexander Graham Bell Association for the Deaf, Michael was among the students he picked to demonstrate incorporating proper speech into everyday life.

"I felt embarrassed because it was hard for me to talk in front of five hundred people," said Michael. "But it was a good experience for me."

Michael has traveled, too, visiting his grandparents in southern California and his great-grandparents in Wisconsin. While with his grandparents, Michael toured Universal Studios and enjoyed Disneyland. He earns extra spending money, for his trips and other things, by baby-sitting for his next-door neighbors.

When it is time for college, he hopes to be able to enter an excellent school.

"I don't know what major I will choose," he said. "But it will probably be math, science, or social studies."

"Hearing-impaired people can achieve their goals, despite the obstacles in their way," Michael said. "I think it is important to be involved with hearing people. Being involved is a challenge to both deaf and hearing. It's worth the effort."

Near-Death Experience Gives Student Courage to Go On

Patty

**Taipei, Taiwan
Harrison-
Chilhowee Baptist
Academy
Knoxville,
Tennessee
Class of 1987**

Patty Pei-Lin Lee, along with her brother, was struck by lightning when she was a young high school student. Her brother died. Patty almost died, too. She remembers vividly her near-death experience.

"My head hurt so much that it seemed ready to explode," she said. "My body became very weak. All of a sudden, I heard a beautiful clear bell ring from heaven. Then someone talked to me in my spirit and told me not to give up. I had to live for my parents and sister because they needed me. I had to be patient with the pain."

Then Patty opened her eyes and found herself in the hospital.

"I realized that the voice that I had heard was God," she said. "He saved me and gave me new life again."

The experience changed Patty's life.

"I believe in Jesus and I am a Christian. Now my life is full of joy and peace," she said. "Whenever I have problems, I trust in God."

That trust has comforted Patty as she pursued her studies in a land far away from that of her parents. Patty came to the United States because the large classes at her school in her native Taiwan could not accommodate a hearing-impaired student.

"Here in the United States, my interpreters enable me to understand everything that the teachers say," she said.

Her first challenge was learning English. She did, learning it well enough to get a medal for the highest grade-point average one year. At graduation from Harrison-Chilhowee Baptist Academy, Patty received the Outstanding Academic Achievement Award and graduated fourth in her class. She was the only deaf student in her graduating class.

"You might say I'm trilingual," said Patty, who can communicate in her native Chinese, as well as English and American Sign Language.

As a member of the International Club at Harrison-Chilhowee, Patty had friends from Japan, Thailand, Zimbabwe, and Ethiopia.

"Living with other students in the dorm

and participating in the International Club gave me an opportunity to learn about different cultures," said Patty.

In high school, her favorite subject was math. She earned an award for the highest grade in algebra in her freshman class, and participated in local math bowls throughout her high school years.

"Math was easy for me," she said. "It was nice to have a good break from reading English all day. I enjoyed the opportunity to work with numbers. "

She loves to play the piano, too.

"I practice very hard, but playing the piano is relaxing and enjoyable for me," said Patty.

Patty is an artist. Her favorite medium is pen and ink, but she likes using watercolors, too. She received art awards during her freshman and sophomore years.

"I enjoy the freedom of self-expression in the fine arts," she said.

Patty is now a student at California State University at Northridge, majoring in interior design.

All of a sudden I heard a beautiful clear bell ring from heaven. Then someone talked to me in my spirit and told me not to give up."

"Ten years from now, I hope to be working in the interior design field," she said. "I also have a dream of helping deaf people in Taiwan. There are many of them—and I understand the difficulties they face."

Patty believes that deaf people need to read newspapers, magazines, and books every day to keep pace with hearing people.

"My parents and I want to encourage deaf young people to have patience and perseverance," she said. "Then they will be successful."

Computer Enthusiast Writes Coach to Join AFL

Justin

**Chico, California
Chico Junior High
School
Chico, California
Class of 1992**

I would like to be the first deaf person to achieve unimaginable goals in computer science. I would like to participate in medical research that would help other deaf people. In America, I have a choice of careers and the opportunity to go as high as I want in education.

My parents and grandparents have helped me to accept my deafness with positive determination. All the members of my family sign, and my grandmother is an interpreter. My little sister, who is hearing, learned to sign before she learned to talk. When she was in fifth grade, she had a ninth-grade vocabulary. My parents think that knowing how to sign helped her to be so far ahead of the other students.

I started to read when I was very young. I have a special interest in math, too. When I was in fifth grade, I took some tests that showed I was gifted in math. I started using the computer in my elementary school.

I participated in a special program at the N-Energy Testing Center in Phoenix, Arizona, to try to improve my hearing. I went to two six-week sessions and worked with a computer-controlled energy machine and my own body energy. The program is still being tested, but when I completed the program, my audiogram showed a small improvement in my hearing in the speech range. The doctors hope that this program will help other deaf people in the future.

I have moved a lot and attended schools in Oklahoma, Iowa, Arizona, and California. I was in an oral program in Oklahoma, and I learned Signing Exact English in Iowa.

Despite all these changes, I have been involved in sports and clubs. I served as president of the Future Farmers of America for two years. I was on soccer, football, track, and baseball teams. I have also been a member of the Boy Scouts and I have attended numerous church activities.

When I moved to California, I made many new friends. Last year, I was voted

I *would like to be the first deaf person to achieve unimaginable goals in computer science. I would like to participate in medical research that would help other deaf people."*

the Most Humorous Boy in Chico Junior High School. Recently, I became a member of the National Honor Society.

I am working to become a good enough football player to make the National Football League. For a few years, I have corresponded with Barry Sweitzer, head coach at Oklahoma University. He sent me pamphlets and a personal letter encouraging me to set my goals and work hard. During one football game, I broke my arm in two places and had to take physical therapy for seven months.

Ten years from now, I hope to work in the field of computer science and make new discoveries that will help other deaf people.

I realize that I will encounter difficulties, but I know that God has given me capabilities that are special, and, with His help, I can overcome any difficulties. I like who I am.

The Feel of Success

Angela

**Austin, Texas
Texas School for
the Deaf
Austin, Texas
Class of 1992**

"It feels wonderful to be successful," said Angela Campion, a student at Texas School for the Deaf (TSD). She should know. Angela's participation in sports has brought her lots of fun and lots of success. She played both forward and goalie on a hearing soccer team in the South Austin League. She played on the volleyball, track, basketball, and tennis teams at TSD. She also won a participation trophy for swimming on her neighborhood team and a second-place trophy for playing tennis.

"I really love to play any sport," said Angela. "It is so much fun to compete."

This spring, she played on a softball team for the first time. Angela and one of her friends were the only two deaf girls on the team. The team won second place, and Angela received a trophy.

"When I was young," she said, "I always thought that I couldn't be on a team with hearing children, but now I find out that the hearing team members are the same as I am. At first, I was afraid, but I learned that it wasn't hard. All that is different is that I can't hear."

In school, Angela's favorite subject is American History.

"I like to learn about my country's past," she said.

She enjoys her class in earth science, too. In her language class, she received an award for bringing all her homework in on time.

Angela also earned thirteen badges—Community Health and Safety, Tending Toddlers, Local Lore, Art in the Home, Folk Arts, Dabbler, Finding Your Way, Outdoor Cook, Outdoor Fun, and four more badges for selling cookies—in Girl Scouts. She also learned about how to take care of herself when camping and what to do if someone got hurt.

"I love camping with friends and family," she said. "Camping is fun."

She has enjoyed riding horses since she was seven years old.

Angela loves to travel and has visited many states, including California, Arizona,

When I was young, I always thought that I couldn't be on a team with hearing children, but now I find out that the hearing team members are the same as I am. At first, I was afraid, but I learned that it wasn't hard. All that is different is that I can't hear."

Oregon, Colorado, Nevada, New Mexico, Idaho, and Utah.

"I travel with my family on vacation just for fun," she said.

She hopes to travel to the eastern states soon.

"Traveling is a short-term goal for me," she said. "I plan to visit Arkansas, Tennessee, Kentucky, Virginia, Washington, D.C., Alabama, Mississippi, and Louisiana. I will

have a lot of fun achieving this goal."

Long-term goals include going to California State University at Northridge or Gallaudet University and becoming a physical education teacher—who lives in California in her very own house.

"I want to encourage deaf students to be active in sports," said Angela. "In sports, hearing and deaf people can compete and have fun together."

Frequent Moves Don't Stop Student from Achieving in Sports, Arts, and Academics

Heidi

Austin, Texas
Texas School for the Deaf
Austin, Texas
Class of 1992

Heidi Vincent, an honor roll student at Texas School for the Deaf (TSD), finally settled in Austin, Texas, after changing schools nine times by the time she was in eighth grade. Heidi loves drawing and plans to work in the Peace Corps.

You have moved around a lot. Can you tell us where you have lived?

My family has lived in California, Oregon, Washington, Alaska, and Minnesota. I have gone to nine different schools. Now we live in Austin, Texas.

Is your family hearing?

My parents are deaf and I have two deaf brothers. My baby sister is hearing.

Do you like school?

Oh, yes! I always have good behavior. In Minnesota, I won a ribbon for good behavior in the dorm. At TSD, teachers have parties for students who obey the rules and have a good attitude. They give us snacks,

show videos, or invite a group to perform for us. I've never missed one.

How about academics?

I made the Gold Honor Roll six times this year, which means I had a grade-point average between 90 and 100. This is my second year at TSD, so it makes me feel proud to be on the honor roll.

What is your favorite subject?

My favorite subject is art. I especially enjoy making pottery and working with clay. I enjoy painting and drawing, too. It's fun to be creative.

What kinds of things do you draw?

I like to draw animals. Some of my drawings are cute and some are far out. I wrote two reports and designed covers for them. The titles were "One of My Best Vacations" and "My Life in Alaska."

Do you enjoy sports? Which ones?

I enjoy many different sports. I love to play

tennis. And I would like to become a skilled tennis player. I play center on our school's girls' basketball team. I am also on the volleyball and track teams. I like to swim and watch baseball games, too.

Describe your work with Student Council.

People come to the Student Council with their suggestions and problems. Last year we helped raise money to buy car seats for babies and art supplies for children in the hospital. The Student Council also surprised each teacher with a piece of cake and a flower.

Have you been involved in activities with hearing people?

Oh yes! I was on a softball team with hearing girls. There were communication breakdowns at times, but we got along fine and became friends. We also won second place.

What do you think you'll be doing ten years from now?

I want to go to college and then join the Peace Corps. I would like to travel to Europe and other countries and live in Australia.

Do you have any advice for other deaf teens?

Get involved. Socialize with hearing people. I made friends. You can, too.

M*y favorite subject is art. I especially enjoy making pottery and working with clay. I enjoy painting and drawing, too. It's fun to be creative."*

Student Hears Bells—and Lots More—Courtesy of Cochlear Implant

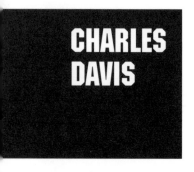

Charlie

**Sanger, Texas
Denton High
School
Denton, Texas
Class of 1989**

In 1984, Charlie Davis, a student at Denton High School, became the first boy in Denton County, Texas, to receive a cochlear implant. Suddenly, he could hear the school bell, feet stamping, dogs barking, the typewriter, the car horn, and his name when someone yelled it. As he did chores after school on his family's farm, he was excited to hear the cow *moo*.

"The implant doesn't make me a hearing person," said Charlie. "I still use sign language and have interpreters in my classes. But it helps me to have more self-confidence."

His favorite classes are history, biology, chemistry, and algebra. As a junior, he took Spanish for the first time and loved it. He has been on the honor roll for three years.

"My teachers are terrific," said Charlie, who was nominated and elected to the Leadership Class of 1988-1989. "I really love my school."

During his senior year, Charlie was elected to the Student Council. The Student Council, cooperating with the Twin Lakes Hospital, promoted a Hugs Not Drugs program. The hospital presented each person on the Student Council with a T-shirt in recognition of their efforts.

A member of the International Arts Club, Charlie drew a picture of a Celebrity Eurosport Sedan that won third place in the regional competiton and second place in the state competition. Charlie also helped with the bonfire at homecoming and worked on the yearbook staff.

Charlie cannot participate in many sports because of his cochlear implant, so he works part-time at Skaggs Alpha Beta, a local grocery store. Charlie does enjoy horseback riding, though, which he describes as easy, but dangerous. Once Charlie fell off his horse and hit his head so sharply he lost his memory.

Charlie is a member of the Grace Bible Church. He went to the World Baptist Youth Conference, near Dallas, Texas.

After he graduates, Charlie wants to major in business and accounting at Gallaudet University, in Washington, D.C. He

I will work to see that services for deaf people are improved. I will also encourage deaf people to become leaders. My main goal is to help other deaf people."

hopes to work as an accountant and be active in his community.

"I will work to see that services for deaf people are improved," he said. "I will also encourage deaf people to become leaders. My main goal is to help other deaf people."

His advice to other students is: "Try your best in activities and subjects that you enjoy—and have fun!"

Scholar and Author Loves to Play the Piano

Holly

**Temple, Texas
Temple High
School
Temple, Texas
Class of 1988**

Holly Corbin is already an author. The *A* student from Temple High School, Temple, Texas, has her own book, *The Beginning,* available at her school library. Written as part of her senior creative writing class, *The Beginning* is a collection of Holly's poems, short stories, and plays, as well as a novel.

An avid student, Holly, a member of the National Honor Society, will graduate in the top ten percent of her class of 500 students at Temple High.

"That honor came through hard work and determination," she said. "Perhaps I work harder than others because of my deafness."

She loves reading, writing, and playing the piano and guitar.

"Maybe it seems unrealistic for a deaf person to play the piano," she said, "but my grandmother taught me and she made it fun for me. I feel the vibrations through the keys, and I can hear the piano a little when I use my hearing aid."

Holly has won numerous awards in piano competitions and sometimes she makes up her own songs.

Holly also enjoys computer programming and is a member of her school computer club. She belongs to the University Inter-scholastic League (UIL), the Journalism Club, and the UIL Spelling Club, too. The National Honor Society earned money for the Heart Fund this year by jumping rope for many hours. Holly received a Jump for Heart certificate for her participation.

"Clubs help students by giving us opportunities to practice skills, compete, and enrich our minds," she said.

Holly works part-time, assisting her aunt with her restaurant. She helps to prepare meals, serve customers, and clean the kitchen.

Born in Iowa, Holly moved to Texas with her family when she was 12 years old. She has two younger brothers, one of whom is deaf. She entered the gifted and talented program and the deaf education program in seventh grade.

"Knowing that I can do what I have done so far tells me that other deaf students can do the same."

Holly hopes to go to Temple Junior College and become a computer programmer or writer.

"Knowing that I can do what I have done so far tells me that other deaf students can do the same," she said. " They won't fail if they concentrate on motivating themselves toward success. Deaf students should use their uniqueness to their advantage."

"Keep Trying... Always Do Your Best"

Jenefer

Woods Cross, Utah
Millcreek Junior High School
Bountiful, Utah
Class of 1991

Jenefer Welch, a student at Millcreek Junior High School in Bountiful, Utah, was named the Outstanding Junior High School student from her school by the Alexander Graham Bell Association for the Deaf at its speech fair. Jenefer wants to become an elementary school teacher.

How long have you been in public school?

I've been in public school since second grade.

What is your favorite subject?

Art. I love to draw. Usually I draw with pencils, but now I'm learning to paint, too.

Are you a member of any clubs? What are some of your activities?

I am a member of the home economics club. We raise money for special supplies for our school. I won a poster and two coupons to use in an amusement center because of my participation in the fund-raising project.

Have you won any awards?

Oh, yes! I was named Outstanding Junior High School Student from my school at a banquet of the Alexander Graham Bell Association for the Deaf last year. I introduced one of the main speakers at the banquet, too.

Do you play sports?

I play basketball and volleyball on the teams sponsored by my church.

Are you active in your church?

Very much so. I go to the Church of Jesus Christ of Latter Day Saints. It's very important to me.

Do you do volunteer work?

Yes. I am a member of the Young Women's Organization at my church. This year, we raised money for a children's medical center in Salt Lake City. I also collected donations for the American Cancer Society.

Do you have any hobbies?

I love to go to my uncle's house and ride his horse. I like to ride my bike, too, for fun and exercise. I also do some baby-sitting.

Are you the only deaf person in your family?

No, my younger brother is deaf. But my sister, who is also younger than I, is hearing. I'm glad she's hearing. If I don't hear something, she repeats it. She explains things to me, too. I don't know what I'd do without her.

What are your goals?

I want to go to college, get married in a temple, and have two children. And I see myself as an elementary school teacher.

Do you have any advice for other deaf students?

My advice is to keep trying...and always do your best.

I *was named Outstanding Junior High School Student from my school at a banquet of the Alexander Graham Bell Association for the Deaf last year."*

CHERI
LYN
KARREN

At School, In Home, Student Lives a Life of Service

Cheri

**Bountiful, Utah
Bountiful High
School
Bountiful, Utah
Class of 1987**

By the time she was a senior in high school, Cheri Karren had already begun a life of service to others. The oldest child in her family and a member of the Church of Jesus Christ of Latter Day Saints, Cheri works as a kitchen helper in a retirement home and cleans house for a woman in her community. She baby-sits, too, and some of her young charges are twins.

"I get along well with people, especially children," said Cheri. "I want to make a contribution to others by working with elementary-age children in a resource program."

At Bountiful High School in Bountiful, Utah, where she goes to school, Cheri is the historian for the club known as BADD—Braves against Drugs and Drinking. As a BADD student, Cheri and her fellow club members travel to other schools giving presentations that encourage students not to use drugs or alcohol. In 1985, Cheri chaired the Organizations against Drugs and Drinking Conference. Also, she partici-

pated in a Psycho-Social Drama Summer Governor's Workshop, working with the local mental health center to help individuals who have problems, such as drug abuse.

Cheri has other interests too. She is on the Bountiful High School swim team, as well as the city swim team.

At the Swim and Tennis Club meet, she placed first in the 100-meter freestyle, 50-meter backstroke, and 50-meter breaststroke. She also placed second in the 50-meter freestyle, fourth in the 100-meter backstroke, and fifth in the 100-meter freestyle in a competition sponsored by McDonald's.

Cheri enjoys creative endeavors and has taken classes in dance, tole painting, and piano. Cheri believes that cooking is an art form. She won second place at the county fair for her lemon bread.

Cheri has traveled extensively throughout the United States and eastern Canada. She likes to listen to music, bike, bowl, roller skate, ice skate, hike, and go to movies and sporting events.

I *get along well with people, especially children. I want to make a contribution to others by working with elementary-age children in a resource program."*

This fall, Cheri will attend Utah State University at Logan. She plans to earn a bachelor of science degree in education and a master's degree in audiology.

"By the end of ten years, I should be well into my career as a resource teacher," she said.

She can imagine herself getting married, having at least two children, and planning many family activities.

Cheri encourages deaf young people to enjoy life to the fullest and stay close to their families. She reminds them to "Please stay away from drugs and alcohol. I've seen what drugs and alcohol can do," said Cheri, "and the results are not pleasant."

"Don't restrict yourself to the world of sign language," she added. "There is much to experience out there." She herself doesn't know how to sign but she said that she intends to learn.

"Don't be afraid to be yourself," said Cheri.

LINDA DIANE ORTIZ

"Go for It!"

Diane

**Las Cruces,
New Mexico
Las Cruces
High School
Las Cruces,
New Mexico
Class of 1989**

Diane Ortiz, a student at Las Cruces High School, in Las Cruces, New Mexico, did not accept defeat when she was turned down for cheerleading. Instead Diane went out for track, worked hard, handled her disappointments—and continued on her way to success.

When did you first go out for track?

When I was in fifth grade. I won first, second, third, fourth, and fifth place for running short distances. I ran the 50-yard dash and the 100-yard dash.

Did you like track?

I liked track because I met many students my age and running was fun. I ran track through seventh grade. The ribbons I won were not as good, compared with the ones I had won in elementary school. I had to compete with more students. In eighth grade, I didn't make the team. I was disappointed. But life goes on.

Did you stop running track?

No, I didn't. In high school, I ran track again. We had hard workouts, but it was worth it. I won several ribbons and certificates of merit for short-distance sprinting.

Do you only do short-distance sprinting?

No. I ran cross-country, though sometimes I wanted to give it up because I never came in first or second. Often, I was last. At first I didn't like it because it was so different from track. But running cross-country helped me to improve my running overall. When the track season came, I was more confident and improved my times. During my junior year, I received a trophy at the end of the season. It was the most exciting time of the whole year for me!

Were you born deaf?

I was born hard-of-hearing, but my family didn't know it until I was about three years old. At that time, I started to learn signs. I have several deaf friends and I am glad I

90

know how to communicate with them. I wear two hearing aids. The hearing aids help me a lot in my classes.

Did you go to special classes for hard-of-hearing students?

I went to a class for hearing-impaired students at New Mexico State University when I was in kindergarten. The next year, my parents had to decide whether I should go to a public school or a school for the deaf. They decided to keep me in a public school so I could live at home.

Did you like public school?

In elementary school, I had a good time because I had hearing-impaired friends and an understanding teacher. When I entered junior high school, I was nervous and scared. At first I couldn't find my locker or my classes. I didn't have any trouble finding my hearing-impaired classes, though, because they were all in the same room.

How were your classes?

In eighth grade, I asked my teacher to put me in more classes with the hearing students. I didn't feel that I was learning as much being in the same classroom with the same students all the time. The next year I had more classes with the hearing students. I had a lot of homework, but it was neat. I am glad I go to public school because it is a challenge to compete with hearing students.

Where did you work last summer?

Last summer I got a job through the summer youth program and worked at the White Sands Missile Range. I had a 45-minute bus ride each way to work. I liked what I did—typing, copying, filing, and working on computers—and everyone was nice to me, but I did not like the long commute.

What college do you want to go to?

I would like to go to college near home, but I may go to Gallaudet University. It will be very hard for me to leave home. My family and I are very close and I haven't been away from home very much. But since I want to be educated and independent, I must grasp any opportunity I can.

How did you feel growing up with a hearing impairment?

At times I felt cheated. I wanted to be a normal hearing person. Maybe I even felt jealous of my sisters. As time went on, I realized that I have to be my own person. I have my own personality and my own judgment. We must accept who we are.

Do you have any words of encouragement for other hearing-impaired students?

Just be yourself. Work hard. And you will be rewarded.

At times I felt cheated. I wanted to be a normal hearing person. Maybe I even felt jealous of my sisters. As time went on, I realized that I have to be my own person. I have my own personality and my own judgment. We must accept who we are."

DUE DATE